Make Ahead
FREEZER
MEALS
FOR THE SLOW COOKER

65 QUICK & EASY SLOW COOKER RECIPES FOR THE BUSY HOME CHEF

ERIN CHASE

Published by FreezEasy Media, via CreateSpace.

ISBN 10: 1720358087
ISBN 13: 978-1720358084

For general information about our workshops, products and services, or to obtain technical support, please contact our Customer Care Team at support@freezeasy.com.

For more great recipes and resources, visit www.myfreezeasy.com.

FREE ONLINE WORKSHOP

Want to spend less time in the kitchen, and more time enjoying other things in life? Need dinner to "take care of itself"? Want to personalize and customize a freezer meal plan - with recipes your family will love?

MyFreezEasy will do all the heavy lifting for you! In a matter of seconds, our apps will pull together your freezer meal recipes, shopping lists, step-by-step instructions and printable labels for your meals. Load up your freezer with make-ahead meals and dinnertime will be a breeze.

In this free online workshop, you'll learn just about everything you need to know about freezer cooking and how it can transform your family's dinner experience.

Sign up for free at: www.myfreezeasy.com/workshop

TABLE OF CONTENTS

How Freezer Cooking
Helps Me Survive This Busy Mom Life

Freezer cooking and the "fast food at home" philosophy of MyFreezEasy has saved me from the drive thru - take out - dining out temptation on dozens (hundreds!?) of occasions! I'm not opposed to the drive thru or take out or dining out, but I do think those meals out on the town should be planned and part of your budget. Getting meals that hold up in the freezer and cook easily in the slow cooker has helped keep me out of the drive thru and eating more meals at home that are healthier and more frugal.

Recently, I found myself at the pediatrician's office with the last appointment of the day. I generally have a 'no last appointment of the morning or afternoon' policy with doctor's offices, because you end up waiting while they catch up from falling behind throughout their visits. But that was the only slot I could get that day for a son whom I suspected had strep throat.

So I'm still sitting in the waiting room at 4:50pm, waiting to see the doctor. At that point, I knew it would be 6pm before we got home, and I'm normally in the kitchen from 5 - 6 pm to prep dinner or reheat a freezer meal. That particular day, I was starting to worry. The temptation to hit the local burger joint on my way home was getting stronger. And just as I was adding up what that drive thru bill might cost, my husband texted that he was on his way home from work.

PHEW! I quickly texted back and asked if he'd be able to get dinner going in the skillet. He said he didn't have anything pressing when he got home, so I shot back the play-by-play on how to thaw and reheat some sloppy joe meat from the freezer.

When I finally arrived home after the strep test (it was positive) and buzzing through to pick up the prescription, it was 6pm. And it smelled amazing in the house, and I just scooped together some sloppy joes, cut up some fruit, grabbed some chips and dinner was served. Total cost of the meal was probably around $5-$6 for all of us. (I'm a ninja sale and deals grocery shopper!)

I was able to save dinner that night, without having to spend $40 in the drive thru!

Another example comes from this past flu season. In 2018, the flu season was exceptionally rough and it hit our family twice - once with each strain. We ended up having a sick kid home from school and activities for 7 weeks in a row, with a brief reprieve in between the 2 strains.

I did my best to keep the sick ones quarantined, keep the house clean and disinfected, plus the time and energy spent nursing them back to health - I was exhausted. There was little energy left for dinner.

It was during those weeks that we'd have back-to-back-to-back freezer meals because they require little thought and little time and little energy to get onto the table.

Another great way to make freezer to slow cooker meals work in your favor is to take a peek at your weekly schedule and figure out which day/days you need help with dinner, or which days you have activities and appointments that keep you away from home and out of the kitchen from 5-6 pm, when you would otherwise be doing meal prep. Make those your "standing freezer to slow cooker meal days."

For the past 2 years, our third son has had an appointment at 5 pm every Monday with the occupational therapist. Her office is about a 20 minute drive, so we are away from home from 4:30ish to 6:30ish every Monday. I'm unable to be home, in the kitchen making a 'fresh meal' for dinner, so I let the slow cooker do the hard work for me. Every-single-Monday. Without fail. For the past tow years, I've been making freezer meals work for me, around our busy schedule, and that has been a lifesaver and money saver too.

Freezer meals and specifically "freezer to slow cooker meals" play such an important role in a busy mom's kitchen. They help keep dinner on the table night after night, even when life is busy, fast, hectic and chaotic. It's such a blessing having freezer meals "on backup" for the nights each week when you need them.

They also help you stay "one step ahead" with both the prepping and the cooking. This helps keep me balanced in my mental energy, eliminating the 'what's for dinner' question, plus it helps keep me on schedule with getting dinner on the table. It's so much easier for me to punch busy in the face when I have dinner "on demand" in the freezer.

Again, the idea and goal of these types of meals is to prep make-ahead meals and keep them in your freezer, to reheat or cook them quickly at a later time. My preferred method is to double 5 recipes, which gets me 10 meals into the freezer in one session. We have built the MyFreezEasy recipes, web app and mobile apps to reflect this philosophy and strategy. You'll find 2 sets of MyFreezEasy freezer meal plans at the end of this cookbook.

Because it really is the easiest and best way to do "fast food at home."

Next, let's talk about the ins and outs of "freezer to slow cooker recipes" and best practices for preparing them for the freezer, and cooking them after being frozen.

About Freezer to Slow Cooker Meals

Slow cooker meals are my favorite type of meal because they are easy to get ready for the freezer, and easy to get going on a busy weekday morning. Even amidst the chaos that ensues in our kitchen every morning, I can still get a slow cooker meal started before heading out for the day.

We are typically 'wheels out' at 7:15 am every morning. The boys know that the wheels roll out of the garage at 7:15. And they do a great job getting themselves ready. They get their backpacks packed, lunch boxes packed (I still help and oversee the younger boys!), correct uniform on, projects in hand, etc.

What happens just before 'wheels out' is akin to a three-ring circus. The busy-ness and movement in the kitchen is mind boggling. But somehow it all works out, some days more smoothly than others.

It starts with coffee (for me). And ends with the "sweep out" and reminders to get everything you need for the day before we leave for the day.

In between there's packing lunches, packing snacks, refilling water bottles, pulling a slow cooker meal from the freezer and adding to a bowl of warm water in the sink, pulling out the slow cooker (the visual reminder on the counter helps me remember to not forget to start it!), pouring of milk, mixing up scrambled eggs, warming bagels, and once partially thawed, getting dinner started in the slow cooker.

It's a flurry of activity. Well, really, it's more like a snowstorm of activity in and around the kitchen. But I don't have trouble getting dinner going, because I've done much of the prep work ahead of time by getting a slow cooker meal into the freezer - to make it fast and simple in the busy morning rush.

Sometimes a few of these activities will happen the evening before, but usually they happen in the morning.

Here's how to get a Freezer to Slow Cooker Meal into the freezer during a prep session:

- **Gather list of freezer to slow cooker recipes** from this cookbook.
- **Jot out what you need from the store.** I suggest doubling all the ingredients and making 2 meals worth of each recipe - it's the fastest, simplest way to get lots of meals prepared in a short amount of time.
- **Shop one afternoon or evening.** Get to the store on day and prepare your meals the next! Pro tip there!
- **Prepare your meals for the freezer.** Add the different ingredients for the meals into baggies or containers and stack them into the freezer.

Note: Use the recipes lists, shopping lists and freezer meal prep instructions at the back of this cookbook!

Here's how to get a freezer meal into the slow cooker:

- **Pull bag from freezer and place in a bowl of warm water.** I usually do this in the sink or next to sink. If you plan to leave the bowl in the water longer than 15-20 minutes, you need to place it in the fridge to keep the food at a safe temperature while thawing.
- **Dump the meal into the slow cooker.** You just need it to thaw long enough to separate the contents from bag (usually only 5-10 minutes), so you can easily get the frozen ingredients into the slow cooker.
- **Cook from partially thawed for at least 8 hours.** If the cooking time is less than 8 hours, you'll want to cook it from completely thawed out.
- **Add ½ cup water or broth.** If you slow cooker "runs hot," add a little extra liquid. (More on that in the next section.
- **Add remaining ingredients.** If called for, swirl in any other ingredients at the end of the cooking cycle. These ingredients are typically pasta, cornstarch, or creams. Cornstarch really needs that time to thicken the sauce, whereas a cream could be added just before serving. In order to set yourself up for success, I recommend setting a timer or reminder for this type of task.

Now that you have a sense of the step-by-step, let's chat briefly about the different types of recipes we include here and a few important notes about them.

Tips for Our Freezer to Slow Cooker Recipes

First off, if your slow cooker tends to dry out food or "run hot" then it's losing more steam or liquid than another model or brand. You'll want to make a note of how much liquid is in the ingredient list and add additional water or broth to compensate for the liquid loss. You won't need to add more than 1/4 to 1/2 cup. Know that some meats (chicken, beef) will release quite a bit of liquid on their own as they cook, but other meats (seafood and pork) won't release as much. If you aren't going to be home, add a little extra liquid to be safe. If you are going to be home, set a timer for half of the cooking time and check to see if you need to add any liquid.

Some of the recipes call for cream of mushroom soups and others have you make a homemade version of cream of mushroom soup. You can swap out 2-3 cups of homemade cream of mushroom soup for a 10 oz. can plus milk. If you wish to make your own cream of mushroom soup, visit 5dollardinners.com and search "homemade cream of mushroom sauce."

Also, some of these meals are "meal starters" - meaning that you'll prepare the base of the meal and add other ingredients to them at the time of cooking. Many of the "add on cook day" ingredients are pantry staples or are freezer friendly, but some you'll need to purchase fresh that week. Here's a short list of those types of ingredients that can be frozen in their packages:

- Corn tortillas
- Flour tortillas
- Shredded cheese

Finally, a few notes about the seafood and fish recipes. Ask the seafood counter to cut the salmon fillet into individual 4 oz. portions for you with their fillet knife. You can leave the skin on to cook them, then remove it after cooking, or you can purchase a fillet without skin. Also, be sure to completely thaw all seafood before slow cooking or cooking with another method. Seafood tends to be more delicate and you don't want it to cook unevenly because it's only partially thawed when you begin the cooking process.

Before we get to the recipes, I wanted to share some other freezer cooking hacks and tips with you.

Other General Freezer Cooking Hacks

MyFreezEasy's freezer cooking meal plans are the perfect solution for the crazy busy home chef who wants to have less stress and less mess when getting dinner on the table.

MyFreezEasy meal plans are designed to help you get 10 meals into your freezer in under one hour, using recipes that can quickly be pulled together into freezer bags or trays. Yes, you can easily put together 10 "dump dinners" in an hour's time.

Even with the fast assembly process and cutting out the dinner hour stress, there are still a number of other essential "HACKS" for putting together MyFreezEasy recipes and meal plans.

1. Let the food cool down completely to reduce risk of freezer burn!

2. Package up and remove as much air possible, if using a plastic baggie. If using a plastic container and freezing liquid, be sure to leave enough headspace at the top, as the liquid will expand as it freezes.

3. "Flat freeze" by pressing the food as flat as possible in the baggie. Then you can stack meals and save space in your freezer. Place a torn piece of wax or parchment paper in between the baggies to prevent them from sticking together and tearing.

4. Thaw completely in the fridge overnight or for up to 2 days if it is 'thick.' If you need the food that day, or within 30 minutes, you can let it soak in a warm bowl of water and it will quickly thaw. The thickness of the baggie or container will determine how long it will take to thaw. When I 'quick-thaw' things, it can take anywhere from 20 minutes to an hour.

Note: If utilizing the quick thaw method, please don't leave raw meat out on the counter in a bowl of warm water. Always let raw meat thaw in the refrigerator to keep it at proper cold temperatures.

5. My recommended "stay in the freezer times" are: up to 6 months for regular fridge freezer, or up to 12 months in deep freezer.

6. Do not (I repeat, do NOT!) shop and prep on the same day. Find a time in your schedule that will allow you to shop the morning/afternoon/evening before, then prep the meals the following day.

7. When meat is on sale at your store, prepare the meals with a plan that will use up all the meat and you'll kill two birds with 1 stone.

- You've saved a ton by stocking up on meat that is on sale.
- You've saved a ton of time and sanity by prepping it all for dinner at once.

8. Use the "Prep Day Shopping List by Recipe" (at the back of this cookbook) when in the checkout lane (or even as you are loading and unloading your cart!) to organize ingredients into specific bags so that when you get home, the ingredients are already grouped together by recipe. The bagger might look at you like you've lost your mind, but you'll be smiling when you get home when it's already organized for your prep & assembly!

9. Drop produce and meats into the fridge in their bags so they are easy to pull out the next day when it's prep time. Leave shelf stable ingredients on the counter, ideally organized in their bags, to make prep set up a cinch.

10. Side Dishes: I leave these very much open and flexible to allow your family to decide which veggies and/or starches are best for your preferences. Make the most of sales and deals on produce and bulk rice or pasta to save big on side dishes too.

Alright, shall we get to the Freezer to Slow Cooker recipes and Slow Cooker freezer meal plans now?!

How to Quickly & Safely Thaw Freezer Meals

Freezer to Slow Cooker Chicken Recipes

Slow Cooker Brown Sugar Chicken

Slow Cooker Butter Chicken

Slow Cooker Chicken Cacciatore

Slow Cooker Chicken Gyros

Slow Cooker Chicken Ropa Vieja

Slow Cooker Creamy Ranch Chicken

Slow Cooker Shredded Hawaiian Chicken Sandwiches

Slow Cooker White Wine Artichoke Chicken

Slow Cooker Brown Sugar Chicken

Yield:	4 servings
Prep Time:	10 minutes
Cook Time:	8 hours in slow cooker

Ingredients for Single Meal

- 4 small boneless chicken breasts
- 1/3 cup cider vinegar
- 1/2 cup brown sugar
- 3 Tbsp soy sauce
- 2 tsp minced garlic
- Salt and pepper
- 2 Tbsp cornstarch
- Garnish: crushed red pepper
- Side: rice
- Side: veggies
- 1 gallon-size freezer baggie

Cooking Directions for Single Meal

1. In a small bowl, whisk together the cider vinegar, brown sugar, soy sauce and minced garlic.
2. Place the chicken breasts in the base of the slow cooker and season with salt and pepper. Then pour the brown sugar sauce around and on top of the chicken.
3. Set on low and cook for 8 hours. With 30 minutes, left in the cooking cycle, swirl the cornstarch with a few Tbsp of water to make a slurry, and then stir it into the sauce. Cook for 30 more minutes to allow sauce to thicken.
4. Cook the rice as directed.
5. Prepare veggies.
6. Serve Slow Cooker Brown Sugar Chicken with rice and veggies.

Freezeasy Meal Prep Directions

- In a small bowl, whisk together 1/3 cup cider vinegar, 1/2 cup brown sugar, 3 Tbsp soy sauce and 2 tsp minced garlic.
- To gallon-size plastic freezer baggie, add the following ingredients:
  - 4 boneless chicken breasts
  - Prepared brown sugar-soy sauce mixture
- Do NOT add the cornstarch before freezing
- Remove as much air as possible and seal. Add label to baggie and freeze.

Freeze & Thaw Instructions

Put baggie in the freezer and freeze up to 6 months in fridge freezer or 12 months in a deep freezer. Thaw in the fridge overnight, or a warm bowl of water for about 20 minutes, before transferring to the slow cooker and cooking on low for 8 hours. Thicken with cornstarch at the end of the cooking cycle, as directed.

Slow Cooker Butter Chicken

Yield: 4 servings
Prep Time: 10 minutes
Cook Time: 8 hours in slow cooker

Ingredients for Single Meal

- 2 large boneless chicken breasts
- 4 boneless chicken thighs
- 1/4 cup butter
- 1 small white onion
- 8 oz. can tomato sauce
- 2 tsp minced garlic
- 1 Tbsp garam masala
- 1 cup chicken stock
- Salt and pepper
- 1 cup heavy cream
- Side: pita bread
- Side: salad
- 1 gallon-size freezer baggie

Cooking Directions for Single Meal

1. Dice the onion.
2. Place the chicken breasts and chicken thighs into the base of the slow cooker and add the butter, diced white onions, tomato sauce, minced garlic, garam masala, chicken stock, salt and pepper on top of the chicken.
3. Set the slow cooker on low and cook for 8 hours. With 30 minutes remaining in the slow cooking cycle, stir in the heavy cream. Once finished cooking, gently shred the chicken with 2 forks and mix into the sauce.
4. Prepare the salad.
5. Serve Slow Cooker Butter Chicken with pita bread and salad.

Freezeasy Meal Prep Directions

- Dice onion.
- Open can of tomato sauce.
- To gallon-size plastic freezer baggie, add the following ingredients:
  - 2 large boneless chicken breasts
  - 4 boneless chicken thighs
  - 1/4 cup butter
  - Diced onion
  - Tomato sauce
  - 2 tsp minced garlic
  - 1 Tbsp garam masala
  - 1 cup chicken stock
  - Salt and pepper
- Note: Do NOT add the heavy cream at this time.
- Remove as much air as possible and seal. Add label to baggie and freeze.

Freeze & Thaw Instructions

Put baggie in the freezer and freeze up to 6 months in fridge freezer or 12 months in a deep freezer. Thaw in the fridge overnight, or a warm bowl of water for about 20 minutes, before transferring to the slow cooker and cooking on low for 8 hours. With 30 minutes remaining in the slow cooking cycle, stir in the heavy cream and then shred chicken as directed.

Slow Cooker Chicken Cacciatore

Yield: 4 servings
Prep Time: 10 minutes
Cook Time: 8 hours in slow cooker

Ingredients for Single Meal

- 4 small boneless chicken breasts
- Salt and pepper
- 1/4 cup red cooking wine
- 1 small white onion
- 1 green bell pepper
- 1 red bell pepper
- 28 oz. can crushed tomatoes
- 2 tsp Italian seasoning
- Side: pasta
- Side: salad
- 1 gallon-size freezer baggie

Cooking Directions for Single Meal

1. Slice the onion. Seed and slice the bell peppers.
2. Place the chicken breasts in the base of the slow cooker and season with salt and pepper. Add red cooking wine around the chicken. Add the sliced onion and bell peppers over the top of the chicken. Then pour the crushed tomatoes over the top and add Italian seasoning.
3. Set slow cooker on low and cook for 8 hours.
4. Cook the pasta, as directed.
5. Prepare the salad.
6. Serve Slow Cooker Chicken Cacciatore over pasta with salad.

Freezeasy Meal Prep Directions

- Slice onion. Seed and slice green and red bell peppers.
- Open can of crushed tomatoes.
- To gallon-size plastic freezer baggie, add the following ingredients:
  - 4 small boneless chicken breasts
  - Salt and pepper
  - 1/4 cup red cooking wine
  - Sliced onion
  - Sliced red and green bell peppers
  - Canned crushed tomatoes
  - 2 tsp Italian seasoning
- Remove as much air as possible and seal. Add label to baggie and freeze.

Freeze & Thaw Instructions

Put baggie in the freezer and freeze up to 6 months in fridge freezer or 12 months in a deep freezer. Thaw in the fridge overnight, or a warm bowl of water for about 20 minutes, before transferring to the slow cooker and cooking on low for 8 hours.

Slow Cooker Chicken Gyros

Yield: 4 servings
Prep Time: 10 minutes
Cook Time: 8 hours in slow cooker

Ingredients for Single Meal

- 4 small boneless chicken breasts
- 1 small white onion
- Salt and pepper
- 1/2 cup lemon juice
- 1/4 cup red wine vinegar
- 2 tsp minced garlic
- 1 tsp oregano
- Garnish: red onion
- Garnish: cucumber slices
- Side: pita bread
- Side: tzatziki sauce
- 1 gallon-size freezer baggie

Cooking Directions for Single Meal

1. Slice the onions into half-moons.
2. In a small bowl, whisk the lemon juice, red wine vinegar, minced garlic and oregano.
3. Place the chicken breasts in the base of the slow cooker and sprinkle the onions around them. Season with a few pinches of salt and pepper. Pour the lemon juice mixture over the top.
4. Set on low and cook for 8 hours. Once cooked, shred the chicken with the sauce. Strain before adding to the pita bread.
5. Warm the pita bread, to help it soften and roll.
6. Prepare the garnish and tzatziki sauce.
7. Serve Slow Cooker Chicken Gyros on pita, with red onion and/or cucumber garnish and tzatziki sauce.

Prepare to Freeze Instructions

- Slice small white onion into half-moons.
- In a small bowl, whisk 1/2 cup lemon juice, 1/4 cup red wine vinegar, 2 tsp minced garlic and 1 tsp oregano.
- To gallon-size plastic freezer baggie, add the following ingredients:
  - 4 boneless chicken breasts
  - Salt and pepper
  - Onion slices
  - Prepared lemon juice marinade
- Remove as much air as possible and seal. Add label to baggie and freeze.

Freeze & Thaw Instructions

Put baggie in the freezer and freeze up to 6 months in fridge freezer or 12 months in a deep freezer. Thaw in the fridge overnight, or a warm bowl of water for about 20 minutes, before transferring to the slow cooker and cooking on low for 8 hours. Shred the chicken with the sauce and strain before adding to the pita bread.

Slow Cooker Chicken Ropa Vieja

Yield:	4 servings
Prep Time:	10 minutes
Cook Time:	8 hours in slow cooker

Ingredients for Single Meal

- 12 boneless chicken thighs
- Salt and pepper
- 1 red bell pepper
- 1 green bell pepper
- 1 small white onion
- 15 oz. can crushed tomatoes
- 1 Tbsp apple cider vinegar
- 1 Tbsp cumin
- 1/2 cup green olives
- Side: rice
- Side: salad
- 1 gallon-size freezer baggie

Cooking Directions for Single Meal

1. Seed and slice the bell peppers. Slice the onion.
2. Place the chicken thighs into the base of the slow cooker and season with salt and pepper. Add the sliced bell peppers and onions, crushed tomatoes, vinegar, cumin and green olives.
3. Set the slow cooker on low and cook for 8 hours. Once finished cooking, shred the chicken with 2 forks and mix into the sauce.
4. Cook the rice, as directed.
5. Spoon the shredded chicken over rice.
6. Prepare the salad.
7. Serve Slow Cooker Chicken Ropa Vieja over rice with salad.

Freezeasy Meal Prep Directions

- Slice onion.
- Seed and slice green bell pepper and red bell pepper.
- Open the can of crushed tomatoes.
- To gallon-size plastic freezer baggie, add the following ingredients:
  - 12 boneless chicken thighs
  - Salt and pepper
  - Sliced green and red bell peppers
  - Sliced onions
  - 15 oz. can crushed tomatoes
  - 1 Tbsp apple cider vinegar
  - 1 Tbsp cumin
  - 1/2 cup green olives
- Remove as much air as possible and seal. Add label to baggie and freeze.

Freeze & Thaw Instructions

Put baggie in the freezer and freeze up to 6 months in fridge freezer or 12 months in a deep freezer. Thaw in the fridge overnight, or a warm bowl of water for about 20 minutes, before transferring to the slow cooker and cooking on low for 8 hours. Once finished cooking, shred the chicken with 2 forks and mix into the sauce.

Special Notes: *Serve with cauli-rice for Paleo/Whole30/Ketogenic meal.*

Slow Cooker Creamy Ranch Chicken

Yield:	4 servings
Prep Time:	20 minutes
Cook Time:	8 hours in slow cooker

Ingredients for Single Meal

- 4 Tbsp butter
- 4 Tbsp all purpose flour
- 2 cups milk
- 1 tsp salt
- Pepper to taste
- 4 oz. baby bella mushrooms
- 4 small boneless chicken breasts
- 1 packet ranch dressing mix
- 4 oz. cream cheese
- Side: dinner rolls
- Side: veggies
- 1 gallon-size freezer baggie

Cooking Directions for Single Meal

1. Wash and chop the mushrooms.
2. In a large skillet or saucepan, melt the butter and then whisk in the flour. Whisking while pouring, add the milk to the flour-butter paste. Whisk milk in vigorously until the flour melts into the milk. Over medium heat, bring to bubbling and the sauce will begin to thicken. Add the salt and chopped mushrooms.
3. Place the chicken in the base of the slow cooker and season with salt and pepper and then add the ranch dressing mix over the top. Pour the homemade cream of mushroom soup over top of the chicken.
4. Set on low and cook for 8 hours. When there is 30 minutes left in the cooking cycle, switch the slow cooker to high and add the cream cheese and let it melt into the sauce.
5. Heat dinner rolls.
6. Prepare veggies.
7. Serve Slow Cooker Creamy Ranch Chicken with dinner rolls and veggies.

Freezeasy Meal Prep Directions

- Wash and chop 4 oz. baby bella mushrooms.
- In a large skillet or saucepan, melt 4 Tbsp butter and then whisk in 4 Tbsp flour. Whisking while pouring, add 2 cups milk to the flour-butter paste. Whisk vigorously until the flour melts into the milk. Over medium heat, bring to bubbling and the sauce will begin to thicken. Add 1 tsp salt and the chopped mushrooms. Set aside and let cool for at least 15 minutes before adding to the freezer baggie.
- To gallon-size plastic freezer baggie, add the following ingredients:
  ◦ 4 small boneless skinless chicken breasts
  ◦ 1 packet ranch dressing mix
  ◦ Prepared cream of mushroom sauce
- Do not add cream cheese to the freezer baggie.
- Remove as much as air as possible and seal.

Freeze & Thaw Instructions

Put baggie in the freezer and freeze up to 6 months in fridge freezer or 12 months in a deep freezer. Thaw in the fridge overnight, or a warm bowl of water for about 20 minutes, before transferring to the slow cooker and cooking on low for 8 hours. With 30 minutes left in the cooking cycle, stir in cream cheese, switch to high and let finish cooking.

Slow Cooker Shredded Hawaiian Chicken Sandwiches

Yield: 4 servings
Prep Time: 10 minutes
Cook Time: 8 hours in slow cooker

Ingredients for Single Meal

- 4 large boneless chicken breasts
- Salt and pepper
- 1/2 cup BBQ sauce
- 2 - 8 oz. cans crushed pineapple
- 1 small red onion
- 8 hamburger buns
- Side: chips
- Side: fruit
- 1 gallon-size freezer baggie

Cooking Directions for Single Meal

1. Chop the red onion.
2. Place the chicken breasts into the base of the slow cooker. Sprinkle a little salt and pepper over the top. Drizzle BBQ sauce over the chicken breasts and then pour the pineapple juices around the chicken breasts, chopped red onion, and the pineapple on top of the chicken.
3. Set on low and cook for 8 hours. Once cooked, pull out the chicken breasts and the pineapple and add to a bowl, then shred with 2 forks and assemble sandwiches.
4. Prepare fruit, as needed.
5. Serve Slow Cooker Shredded Hawaiian Chicken Sandwiches with fruit and chips.

Freezeasy Meal Prep Directions

- Chop 1 small red onion.
- Open 2 cans of crushed pineapple. Do not drain.
- To gallon-size plastic freezer baggie, add the following ingredients:
  - 4 large boneless, skinless chicken breasts
  - Salt and pepper
  - 1/2 cup BBQ sauce
  - Both cans of crushed pineapple
  - Chopped onion
- Remove as much air as possible and seal. Add label to baggie and freeze.

Freeze & Thaw Instructions

Put baggie in the freezer and freeze up to 6 months in fridge freezer or 12 months in a deep freezer. Thaw in the fridge overnight, or a warm bowl of water for about 20 minutes, before transferring to the slow cooker and cooking on low for 8 hours. Once cooked, pull out the chicken breasts and the pineapple and add to a bowl, then shred with 2 forks and assemble sandwiches.

Slow Cooker White Wine Artichoke Chicken

Yield: 4 servings
Prep Time: 10 minutes
Cook Time: 8 hours in slow cooker

Ingredients for Single Meal

- 4 small boneless chicken breasts
- 1 cup white cooking wine
- 1 cup chicken stock
- 15 oz. can artichoke hearts
- 2 Tbsp butter
- 1 Tbsp lemon juice
- Salt and pepper
- 1 Tbsp cornstarch
- Side: pasta
- Side: salad
- 1 gallon-size freezer baggie

Cooking Directions for Single Meal

1. Open and drain the can of artichokes.
2. Place the chicken breasts in the base of the slow cooker and pour the white wine, chicken stock, artichoke hearts, butter, and lemon juice around the chicken. Season with salt and pepper.
3. Set on low and cook for 8 hours. With 30 minutes left in the cooking cycle, whisk in the cornstarch and let sauce thicken as it finishes cooking.
4. Cook the pasta as directed.
5. Prepare salad.
6. Serve Slow Cooker White Wine Artichoke Chicken with over pasta with salad.

Freezeasy Meal Prep Directions

- Open and drain 1 can of artichoke hearts.
- To gallon-size plastic freezer baggie, add the following ingredients:
  - 4 boneless chicken breasts
  - 1 cup white cooking wine
  - 1 cup chicken stock
  - Canned artichoke hearts
  - 2 Tbsp butter
  - 1 Tbsp lemon juice
  - Salt and pepper
- Do NOT add cornstarch to the freezer bag.
- Remove as much air as possible and seal. Add label to baggie and freeze.

Freeze & Thaw Instructions

Put baggie in the freezer and freeze up to 6 months in fridge freezer or 12 months in a deep freezer. Thaw in the fridge overnight, or a warm bowl of water for about 20 minutes, before transferring to the slow cooker and cooking on low for 8 hours. Thicken with cornstarch at the end of the cooking cycle, as directed.

Freezer to Slow Cooker Beef Recipes

Slow Cooker Barbacoa Beef

Slow Cooker Beef Ragu

Slow Cooker Chimichurri Beef Roast

Slow Cooker French Dip Sandwiches

Slow Cooker Italian Beef Sandwiches

Slow Cooker Mississippi Beef Roast

Slow Cooker Mongolian Beef

Slow Cooker Mushroom Pot Roast

Slow Cooker Red Wine Beef Roast

Slow Cooker Russian Shredded Beef Sandwiches

Slow Cooker Santa Fe Beef

Slow Cooker Shredded Beef Tacos with Mango Avocado Salsa

Slow Cooker Simple Baby Beef Stew

Slow Cooker Barbacoa Beef

Yield:	4 servings
Prep Time:	10 minutes
Cook Time:	8 hours in slow cooker

Ingredients for Single Meal

- 3 lb. beef chuck roast
- Salt and pepper
- 1 small white onion
- 1 small chipotle chili
- 1 cup beef stock
- 1/4 cup apple cider vinegar
- 1/4 cup lime juice
- 1 tsp dried oregano
- 1 tsp Adobo seasoning
- 1 tsp ground cumin
- Salt and pepper
- Side: veggies
- Side: rice
- 1 gallon-size freezer baggie

Cooking Directions for Single Meal

1. Chop the white onion. Slice the chipotle chili and remove seeds.
2. Place the beef roast into the base of the slow cooker and season with salt and pepper. Add the chopped onion and sliced chili over the top. Pour the beef stock, cider vinegar, lime juice around the beef roast. Sprinkle the oregano, adobo, and ground cumin over the top.
3. Set the slow cooker on low and cook for 8 hours. Once finished cooking, shred the beef with 2 forks and mix into the sauce. Season with salt and pepper to taste.
4. Cook the rice, as directed.
5. Prepare the veggies.
6. Serve Slow Cooker Barbacoa Beef with rice and veggies.

Freezeasy Meal Prep Directions

- Chop 1 white onion. Slice 1 chipotle chile and remove seeds.
- To gallon-size plastic freezer baggie, add the following ingredients:
  - 3 lb. beef chuck roast
  - Chopped onion
  - Sliced chilis
  - 1 cup beef stock
  - 1/4 cup apple cider vinegar
  - 1/4 cup lime juice
  - 1 tsp dried oregano
  - 1 tsp adobo seasoning
  - 1 tsp ground cumin
- Remove as much air as possible and seal. Add label to baggie and freeze.

Freeze & Thaw Instructions

Put baggie in the freezer and freeze up to 6 months in fridge freezer or 12 months in a deep freezer. Thaw in the fridge overnight, or a warm bowl of water for about 20 minutes, before transferring to the slow cooker and cooking on low for 8 hours. Once finished cooking, shred the beef with 2 forks and mix into the sauce.

Slow Cooker Beef Ragu

Yield: 4 servings
Prep Time: 10 minutes
Cook Time: 8 hours in slow cooker

Ingredients for Single Meal

- 2 lbs. stew beef
- Salt and pepper
- 28 oz. can crushed tomatoes
- 1/4 cup sliced green olives
- 1 cup beef stock
- 2 whole carrots
- 1 Tbsp minced onion
- 1 tsp minced garlic
- 1 tsp dried oregano
- 1 tsp dried rosemary
- 2 Tbsp heavy cream
- Garnish: shredded Parmesan cheese
- Side: pasta
- Side: salad
- 1 gallon-size freezer baggie

Cooking Directions for Single Meal

1. Peel and shred the carrots.
2. Place the stew beef into the base of the slow cooker and season with salt and pepper. Pour the crushed tomatoes, sliced green olives, beef stock, shredded carrots, minced onion, minced garlic, oregano, rosemary and gently stir to combine.
3. Set the slow cooker on low and cook for 8 hours. Once finished cooking, stir in the heavy cream. Garnish sauce with shredded Parmesan cheese.
4. Cook the pasta, as directed.
5. Prepare the salad.
6. Serve Slow Cooker Beef Ragu over pasta with side salad.

Freezeasy Meal Prep Directions

- Peel and shred 2 whole carrots.
- Open can of crushed tomatoes.
- To gallon-size plastic freezer baggie, add the following ingredients:
  - 2 lbs. stew beef
  - Salt and pepper
  - 28 oz. can crushed tomatoes
  - 1/4 cup sliced green olives
  - 1 cup beef stock
  - Shredded carrots
  - 1 Tbsp minced onion
  - 1 tsp minced garlic
  - 1 tsp dried oregano
  - 1 tsp dried rosemary
- Do not add heavy cream to freezer baggie.
- Remove as much air as possible and seal. Add label to baggie and freeze.

Freeze & Thaw Instructions

Put baggie in the freezer and freeze up to 6 months in fridge freezer or 12 months in a deep freezer. Thaw in the fridge overnight, or a warm bowl of water for about 20 minutes, before transferring to the slow cooker and cooking on low for 8 hours. Stir in the heavy cream at the end of cooking.

Special Notes: *Substitution: if your store doesn't sell "stew beef" cut, then you can purchase a 2 lb. beef chuck roast and cut it into 1-inch pieces.*

Slow Cooker Chimichurri Beef Roast

Yield: 4 servings
Prep Time: 10 minutes
Cook Time: 8 hours in slow cooker

Ingredients for Single Meal

- 2 lb. beef chuck roast
- 7 oz. jar chimichurri sauce
- Salt and pepper
- Side: black beans
- Side: rice
- Side: veggies
- 1 gallon-size freezer baggie

Cooking Directions for Single Meal

1. Place the beef roast into the base of the slow cooker and season with salt and pepper. Spread the chimichurri sauce directly over the roast. Note: if you slow cooker "runs hot" and overcooks meat, you might want to add a cup of water or beef broth.
2. Set the slow cooker on low and cook for 8 hours.
3. Cook the rice as directed.
4. Prepare the veggies and black beans.
5. Serve Slow Cooker Chimichurri Beef Roast with rice and beans and side of veggies.

Freezeasy Meal Prep Directions

- To gallon-size plastic freezer baggie, add the following ingredients:
  - 2 lb. beef chuck roast
  - Salt and pepper
  - 1 jar of chimichurri sauce
- Remove as much air as possible and seal. Add label to baggie and freeze.

Freeze & Thaw Instructions

Put baggie in the freezer and freeze up to 6 months in fridge freezer or 12 months in a deep freezer. Thaw in the fridge overnight, or a warm bowl of water for about 20 minutes, before transferring to the slow cooker and cooking on low for 8 hours.

Slow Cooker French Dip Sandwiches

Yield: 4 servings
Prep Time: 10 minutes
Cook Time: 8 hours in slow cooker

Ingredients for Single Meal

- 3 lb. beef roast
- 1 small white onion
- 1 packet dry French onion soup mix
- 1 cup beef stock
- Salt and pepper
- 4 slices Provolone cheese
- 4 bolillo or hoagie rolls
- Side: salad
- 1 gallon-size freezer baggie

Cooking Directions for Single Meal

1. Slice the white onion.
2. Place the beef roast into the base of the slow cooker and add the sliced onions around the beef roast. Sprinkle the dry French onion soup mix around the beef and onions. Pour the beef stock around the edge of the slow cooker. Season with salt and pepper, as desired.
3. Set the slow cooker on low and cook for 8 hours. Once finished cooking, ladle out about 2 cups of the beef stock and onions to use as a dipping sauce. Then, slice or shred the beef roast and serve into the hoagie rolls. Add a slice of Provolone cheese to each sandwich.
4. Prepare the salad.
5. Serve Slow Cooker French Dip Sandwiches with salad.

Freezeasy Meal Prep Directions

- Slice 1 small white onion.
- To gallon-size plastic freezer baggie, add the following ingredients:
  - 3 lb. beef roast
  - Sliced onion
  - 1 packet dry French onion soup mix
  - 1 cup beef stock
  - Salt and pepper
- Remove as much air as you can and seal. Freeze up to 6 months in your fridge freezer or 12 months in a deep freezer.

Freeze & Thaw Instructions

Put baggie in the freezer and freeze up to 6 months in fridge freezer or 12 months in a deep freezer. Thaw in the fridge overnight, or a warm bowl of water for about 20 minutes, before transferring to the slow cooker and cooking on low for 8 hours. Once finished cooking, ladle out about 2 cups of the beef and onions to use as a dipping sauce. Then, slice or shred the beef roast and assemble sandwiches, as directed.

Slow Cooker Italian Beef Sandwiches

Yield: 4 servings
Prep Time: 10 minutes
Cook Time: 8 hours in slow cooker

Ingredients for Single Meal

- 2 lb. beef chuck roast
- Salt and pepper
- 15 oz. can tomato sauce
- 1 green bell pepper
- 1 red bell pepper
- 1 small white onion
- 1 cup pepperoncini peppers
- 1 packet ranch dressing mix
- 4 bolillo or hoagie rolls
- 4 slices Provolone cheese
- Side: salad
- 1 gallon-size freezer baggie

Cooking Directions for Single Meal

1. Seed and slice the green and red bell peppers. Slice the onion.
2. Place the beef roast in the base of the slow cooker and season with salt and pepper. Add the tomato sauce, sliced green and red bell peppers, sliced onions, pepperoncini peppers and Ranch dressing mix.
3. Set the slow cooker on low and cook for 8 hours.
4. Once cooked, shred the meat and veggies with 2 forks and combine with the sauce. Spoon the shredded beef onto the bolillo or hoagie rolls. Add slice of cheese on top and microwave to melt, if needed.
5. Prepare the salad.
6. Serve Slow Cooker Italian Beef Sandwiches with side salad.

Freezeasy Meal Prep Directions

- Seed and slice 1 green and 1 red bell pepper. Slice 1 small white onion.
- Open 1 can of tomato sauce.
- To gallon-size plastic freezer baggie, add the following ingredients:
  - 2 lb. chuck or pot roast
  - Salt and pepper
  - Canned tomato sauce
  - Sliced green bell pepper
  - Sliced red bell pepper
  - Sliced onions
  - 1 cup pepperoncini peppers
  - 1 packet ranch dressing mix
- Remove as much air as possible and seal. Add label to baggie and freeze.

Freeze & Thaw Instructions

Put baggie in the freezer and freeze up to 6 months in fridge freezer or 12 months in a deep freezer. Thaw in the fridge overnight, or a warm bowl of water for about 20 minutes, before transferring to the slow cooker and cooking on low for 8 hours. Once cooked, shred the meat and veggies with 2 forks and combine with the sauce. Spoon the shredded beef onto the bolillo or hoagie rolls and assemble sandwiches, as directed.

Slow Cooker Mississippi Beef Roast

Yield: 4 servings
Prep Time: 10 minutes
Cook Time: 8 hours in slow cooker

Ingredients for Single Meal

- 2 lb. beef chuck roast
- 4 Tbsp butter
- 1 packet ranch dressing mix
- 8 pepperoncini peppers
- 1 tsp pepper
- Side: dinner rolls
- Side: veggies
- 1 gallon-size freezer baggie

Cooking Directions for Single Meal

1. Cut butter into 4 - 1 Tbsp pieces.
2. Place the beef roast in the base of the slow cooker and season with Ranch dressing mix. Add the butter slices and the pepperoncini peppers directly on the roast and sprinkle the pepper on top. Set slow cooker on low and cook for 8 hours.
3. Warm the dinner rolls.
4. Prepare veggies.
5. Serve Slow Cooker Mississippi Mud Beef Roast with veggies and dinner rolls.

Freezeasy Meal Prep Directions

- Cut the butter into 4 - 1 Tbsp pieces.
- To gallon-size plastic freezer baggie, add the following ingredients:
  - 2 lb beef chuck roast
  - 1 packet Ranch dressing mix
  - 4 butter pieces
  - 8 pepperoncini peppers
  - 1 tsp pepper
- Remove as much air as possible and seal. Add label to baggie and freeze.

Freeze & Thaw Instructions

Put baggie in the freezer and freeze up to 6 months in fridge freezer or 12 months in a deep freezer. Thaw in the fridge overnight, or a warm bowl of water for about 20 minutes, before transferring to the slow cooker and cooking on low for 8 hours.

Slow Cooker Mongolian Beef

Yield: 4 servings
Prep Time: 10 minutes
Cook Time: 4 hours in slow cooker

Ingredients for Single Meal

- 1 1/2 lbs. beef strips for stirfry
- 2 Tbsp canola oil
- 2 Tbsp cornstarch
- 2 garlic cloves
- 1 Tbsp minced onion
- 1 tsp minced ginger
- 2/3 cup soy sauce
- 2/3 cup water
- 2/3 cup brown sugar
- 1/2 lb bag shredded carrots
- 1 tsp crushed red pepper
- Garnish: green onion
- Side: rice
- Side: veggies
- 1 gallon-size freezer baggie

Cooking Directions for Single Meal

1. In a small mixing bowl toss the beef with the oil and cornstarch. Place into the base of the slow cooker.
2. In a mixing bowl, whisk together the crushed garlic, minced onion, minced ginger, soy sauce, water and brown sugar. Pour over the beef in the slow cooker. Add the shredded carrots and crushed red pepper over the top.
3. Set on low and cook for 4 hours. If you need to cook it on low for 8 hours, add an extra ½ cup of water.
4. Cook the rice, as directed.
5. Prepare veggies.
6. Serve Slow Cooker Mongolian Beef over rice with veggies and optional green onion garnish.

Freezeasy Meal Prep Directions

- Toss together 1 1/2 lbs. beef strips with 2 Tbsp canola oil and 2 Tbsp cornstarch.
- Whisk together 2 crushed garlic cloves, 1 Tbsp minced onion, 1 tsp minced ginger, 2/3 cup soy sauce, 2/3 cup water, 2/3 cup brown sugar.
- To gallon-size plastic freezer baggie, add the following ingredients:
  - Beef strips coated in cornstarch
  - Prepared sauce
  - Shredded carrots
  - 1 tsp crushed red pepper
- Remove as much air as possible and seal. Add label to baggie and freeze.

Freeze & Thaw Instructions

Put baggie in the freezer and freeze up to 6 months in fridge freezer or 12 months in a deep freezer. Thaw in a warm bowl of water for about 20 minutes, before transferring to the slow cooker and cooking on low for 4 hours.

Slow Cooker Mushroom Pot Roast

Yield: 4 servings
Prep Time: 10 minutes
Cook Time: 8 hours in slow cooker

Ingredients for Single Meal

- 2 lb. beef chuck roast
- Salt and pepper
- 1 small white onion
- 8 oz. sliced white mushrooms
- 10 oz. can cream of mushroom
- 1 cup white cooking wine
- 2 Tbsp Worcestershire sauce
- Side: veggies
- Side: mashed potatoes
- 1 gallon-size freezer baggie

Cooking Directions for Single Meal

1. Slice the onion into half-moons.
2. Place the beef roast into the base of the slow cooker and season with salt and pepper.
3. In a large mixing bowl, whisk together the cream of mushroom soup, white cooking wine and Worcestershire sauce. Then fold in the sliced onion and sliced mushrooms. Pour over the beef roast in the slow cooker.
4. Set the slow cooker on low and cook for 8 hours. Once finished cooking, shred the beef with 2 forks and mix into the sauce.
5. Prepare the veggies.
6. Prepare the mashed potatoes.
7. Serve Slow Cooker Mushroom Pot Roast over mashed potatoes with side of veggies.

Freezeasy Meal Prep Directions

- Slice 1 small onion into half-moons.
- Open the can of cream of mushroom soup.
- To gallon-size plastic freezer baggie, add the following ingredients:
  - 2 lb. beef chuck roast
  - Salt and pepper
  - Sliced onion
  - 8 oz. sliced white mushrooms
  - 10 oz. can cream of mushroom soup
  - 1 cup white cooking wine
  - 2 Tbsp Worcestershire sauce
- Remove as much air as possible and seal. Add label to baggie and freeze.

Freeze & Thaw Instructions

Put baggie in the freezer and freeze up to 6 months in fridge freezer or 12 months in a deep freezer. Thaw in the fridge overnight, or a warm bowl of water for about 20 minutes, before transferring to the slow cooker and cooking on low for 8 hours. Once finished cooking, shred the beef with 2 forks and mix into the sauce.

Slow Cooker Red Wine Beef Roast

Yield: 4 servings
Prep Time: 10 minutes
Cook Time: 8 hours in slow cooker

Ingredients

- 3 lb. beef chuck roast
- Salt and pepper
- 1/4 cup red wine
- 2 tsp minced garlic
- 2 tsp chopped chives
- 3 lb. bag baby potatoes
- 1 cup beef broth
- Side: salad
- 1 gallon-size freezer baggie

Cooking Directions for Single Meal

1. Place the beef chuck roast into the base of the slow cooker and season with salt and pepper. Pour the red wine, minced garlic and chopped chives over the beef roast. Nestle the baby potatoes around the beef roast and then pour in 1 cup beef broth.
2. Set the slow cooker on low and cook for 8 hours.
3. Prepare the salad.
4. Serve Slow Cooker Red Wine Beef Roast and potatoes with side salad.

Freezeasy Meal Prep Directions

- To gallon-size plastic freezer baggie, add the following ingredients:
  - 3 lb. beef roast
  - Salt and pepper
  - 1/4 cup red wine
  - 2 tsp minced garlic
  - 2 tsp chopped chives
  - 3 lb. bag baby potatoes
  - 1 cup beef broth
- Remove as much air as possible and seal. Add label to baggie and freeze.

Freeze & Thaw Instructions

Put baggie in the freezer and freeze up to 6 months in fridge freezer or 12 months in a deep freezer. Thaw in the fridge overnight, or a warm bowl of water for about 20 minutes, before transferring to the slow cooker and cooking on low for 8 hours.

Slow Cooker Russian Shredded Beef Sandwiches

Yield: 4 servings
Prep Time: 10 minutes
Cook Time: 8 hours in slow cooker

Ingredients for Single Meal

- 2 lb. beef chuck roast
- Salt and pepper
- 1 cup Russian salad dressing
- 1 Tbsp minced onion
- 1 tsp garlic powder
- Salt and pepper
- 4 hoagie rolls
- 4 slices Swiss cheese
- Garnish: coleslaw
- Side: fruit
- 1 gallon-size freezer baggie

Cooking Directions for Single Meal

1. Place the beef roast into the base of the slow cooker and season with salt and pepper. Pour the Russian salad dressing over the top and sprinkle the minced onion and garlic powder over the top.
2. Set the slow cooker on low and cook for 8 hours. Once finished cooking, shred the beef with 2 forks and mix into the sauce.
3. Prepare the Coleslaw, and assemble sandwiches with shredded beef, Swiss cheese and Coleslaw.
4. Prepare the fruit.
5. Serve Russian Shredded Beef Sandwiches with side of fruit.

Freezeasy Meal Prep Directions

- To gallon-size plastic freezer baggie, add the following ingredients:
  ◦ 2 lb. beef chuck roast
  ◦ Salt and pepper
  ◦ 1 cup Russian salad dressing
  ◦ 1 Tbsp minced onion
  ◦ 1 tsp garlic powder
  ◦ Do not add rolls, cheese or Coleslaw to freezer baggie.
- Remove as much air as possible and seal. Add label to baggie and freeze.

Freeze & Thaw Instructions

Put baggie in the freezer and freeze up to 6 months in fridge freezer or 12 months in a deep freezer. Thaw in the fridge overnight, or a warm bowl of water for about 20 minutes, before transferring to the slow cooker and cooking on low for 8 hours. Once finished cooking, shred the beef with 2 forks, mix into the sauce, and then prepare sandwiches as directed.

Slow Cooker Santa Fe Beef

Yield:	4 servings
Prep Time:	10 minutes
Cook Time:	8 hours in slow cooker

Ingredients for Single Meal

- 2 lb. beef chuck roast
- Salt and pepper
- 1 packet taco seasoning
- 4 oz. can green chiles
- 1 cup red salsa
- Side: salad
- Side: dinner rolls
- 1 gallon-size freezer baggie

Cooking Directions for Single Meal

1. Place the beef roast into the base of the slow cooker and season with salt and pepper. Sprinkle the taco seasoning over the roast. Pour the green chilies and red salsa over the top.
2. Set the slow cooker on low and cook for 8 hours. Once finished cooking, shred the beef with 2 forks and mix into the sauce.
3. Prepare salad.
4. Warm the dinner rolls.
5. Serve Slow Cooker Santa Fe Beef with salad and dinner rolls.

Freezeasy Meal Prep Directions

- Open 1 can of green chiles.
- To gallon-size plastic freezer baggie, add the following ingredients:
  - 2 lb. beef chuck roast
  - Salt and pepper
  - 1 packet taco seasoning
  - 4 oz. can green chilies
  - 1 cup red salsa
- Remove as much air as possible and seal. Add label to baggie and freeze.

Freeze & Thaw Instructions

Put baggie in the freezer and freeze up to 6 months in fridge freezer or 12 months in a deep freezer. Thaw in the fridge overnight, or a warm bowl of water for about 20 minutes, before transferring to the slow cooker and cooking on low for 8 hours. Once finished cooking, shred the beef with 2 forks and mix into the sauce.

Slow Cooker Shredded Beef Tacos with Mango Avocado Salsa

Yield:	4 servings
Prep Time:	10 minutes
Cook Time:	8 hours in slow cooker

Ingredients for Single Meal

- 1 1/2 lb beef roast
- 1 lime
- 1 tsp ground cumin
- 1 tsp salt and pepper, each
- 1 mango
- 1 lime
- 2 small avocado
- small bunch cilantro
- 12 tortillas, flour or corn
- Side: corn on the cob
- 1 gallon-size freezer baggie

Cooking Directions for Single Meal

1. Place the beef roast in the slow cooker. Squeeze from one lime over the top, then sprinkle with cumin, salt and pepper. Carefully pour 1/2 cup water around the beef roast.
2. Set on low and cook for 8 hours. Once cooked, shred the beef with 2 forks.
3. Before dinner, mix up the diced mango, diced avocado, juice from remaining lime, cilantro and salt and pepper together in a bowl.
4. Add the slow cooked beef into the tortillas and top with the mango-avocado salsa.
5. Prepare corn on the cob.
6. Serve Shredded Beef Tacos with Mango Avocado Salsa and corn on the cob.

Freezeasy Meal Prep Directions

- Halve 1 lime.
- To gallon-size plastic freezer baggie, add the following ingredients:
  - 1 1/2 lb beef roast
  - Juice from 1 lime
  - 1 tsp ground cumin
  - 1 tsp salt and pepper, each
- Note: Do NOT add the fresh produce for the salsa or tortillas to the freezer baggies.
- Remove as much air as possible and seal. Add label to baggie and freeze.

Freeze & Thaw Instructions

Put baggie in the freezer and freeze up to 6 months in fridge freezer or 12 months in a deep freezer. Thaw in the fridge overnight, or a warm bowl of water for about 20 minutes, before transferring to the slow cooker and cooking on low for 8 hours. Once cooked, shred the beef with 2 forks and prepare salsa and tacos, as directed.

Slow Cooker Simple Baby Beef Stew

Yield:	4 servings
Prep Time:	10 minutes
Cook Time:	8 hours in slow cooker

Ingredients for Single Meal

- 2 lbs. stew beef
- 3 lb. bag baby potatoes
- 1 lb. bag baby carrots
- 8 oz. can tomato sauce
- 1 Tbsp minced onion
- 1 tsp minced garlic
- 1 tsp Italian seasoning
- 2 cups beef stock
- Salt and pepper
- Side: dinner rolls
- 1 gallon-size freezer baggie

Cooking Directions for Single Meal

1. To the base of the slow cooker, add the stew beef, baby potatoes, baby carrots, tomato sauce, minced onion, minced garlic, Italian seasoning and beef stock. Season with salt and pepper.
2. Set the slow cooker on low and cook for 8 hours.
3. Prepare the dinner rolls.
4. Serve Slow Cooker Simple Baby Beef Stew with dinner rolls.

Freezeasy Meal Prep Directions

- Open the can of tomato sauce.
- To gallon-size plastic freezer baggie, add the following ingredients:
  - 2 lbs. stew beef
  - 3 lb. bag baby potatoes
  - 1 lb. bag baby carrots
  - 8 oz. can tomato sauce
  - 1 Tbsp minced onion
  - 1 tsp minced garlic
  - 1 tsp Italian seasoning
  - 2 cups beef stock
  - Salt and pepper
- Remove as much air as you can and seal. Freeze up to 6 months in your fridge freezer or 12 months in a deep freezer.

Freeze & Thaw Instructions

Put baggie in the freezer and freeze up to 6 months in fridge freezer or 12 months in a deep freezer. Thaw in the fridge overnight, or a warm bowl of water for about 20 minutes, before transferring to the slow cooker and cooking on low for 8 hours.

Freezer to Slow Cooker Ground Beef Recipes

Slow Cooker BBQ Meatballs

Slow Cooker Beef & Black Bean Chili

Slow Cooker Beef and Vegetable Soup

Slow Cooker Beef Stroganoff

Slow Cooker Cheeseburger Chili

Slow Cooker Chili Mac

Slow Cooker Cowboy Chili

Slow Cooker Creamy Taco Soup

Slow Cooker Layered Enchiladas

Slow Cooker Sweet & Sour Meatballs

Slow Cooker Taco Soup

Slow Cooker BBQ Meatballs

Yield: 4 servings
Prep Time: 10 minutes
Cook Time: 4 hours in slow cooker

Ingredients for Single Meal

- 1 lb. precooked frozen meatballs
- 1/2 cup beef broth
- 1 small white onion
- 15 oz. can crushed pineapple
- 2 cup BBQ sauce
- 1 Tbsp honey
- 1 tsp minced garlic
- Salt and pepper
- Side: rice
- Side: veggies
- 1 gallon-size freezer baggie

Cooking Directions for Single Meal

1. Chop the onion. Open and drain the can of pineapple.
2. To the slow cooker, add the precooked meatballs and chopped onion. Pour the beef broth around the meatballs.
3. In a large mixing bowl, whisk together the crushed pineapple, BBQ sauce, honey and minced garlic. Pour this sauce over the meatballs and onions. Set slow cooker on low and cook for 4 hours.
4. Prepare rice and veggies.
5. Serve Slow Cooker BBQ Meatballs with rice and veggies.

Freezeasy Meal Prep Directions

- Chop 1 small white onion.
- To gallon-size plastic freezer baggie, add the following ingredients:
  - 1 lb. precooked frozen meatballs
  - Chopped onion
  - 15 oz. can crushed pineapple
  - 2 cups BBQ sauce
  - 1 Tbsp honey
  - 1 tsp minced garlic
  - Do NOT add the beef broth before freezing.
- Remove as much air as possible and seal. Add label to baggie and freeze.

Freeze & Thaw Instructions

Put baggie in the freezer and freeze up to 6 months in fridge freezer or 12 months in a deep freezer. Thaw in the fridge overnight, or a warm bowl of water for about 20 minutes. Add the beef broth into the base of the slow cooker, then add the meatballs and sauce. Set on low and cook for 4 hours.

Slow Cooker Beef & Black Bean Chili

Yield: 4 servings
Prep Time: 15 minutes
Cook Time: 8 hours in slow cooker

Ingredients for Single Meal

- 1 lb. ground beef
- 1 Tbsp minced onion
- 1 tsp garlic powder
- 2 - 15 oz. can black beans
- 2 - 15 oz. can tomato sauce
- 2 Tbsp chili powder
- Salt and pepper
- Garnish: shredded cheddar cheese
- Garnish: sour cream
- Side: veggies
- 1 gallon-size freezer baggie

Cooking Directions for Single Meal

1. Brown the ground beef in a large skillet with the minced onion and garlic powder. Drain, if needed, and add to the base of the slow cooker.
2. Stir in the black beans, tomato sauce, chili powder, salt and pepper. Set on low and cook for 8 hours.
3. Prepare the veggies.
4. Serve Slow Cooker Beef & Black Bean Chili with optional garnishes and veggies.

Freezeasy Meal Prep Directions

- Brown the ground beef with 1 Tbsp minced onion and 1 tsp garlic powder. Let cool before adding to freezer baggie.
- Open, drain and rinse 2 cans of black beans.
- Open 2 cans of tomato sauce.
- To gallon-size plastic freezer baggie, add the following ingredients:
  - Browned ground beef
  - 2 – 15 oz. cans black beans, drained and rinsed
  - 2 – 15 oz. cans tomato sauce
  - 2 Tbsp chili powder
  - Salt and pepper to taste
- Remove as much air as possible and seal. Add label and freeze.

Freeze & Thaw Instructions

Put baggie in the freezer and freeze up to 6 months in fridge freezer or 12 months in a deep freezer. Thaw in the fridge overnight, or a warm bowl of water for about 20 minutes, before transferring to the slow cooker and cooking on low for 8 hours.

Slow Cooker Beef and Vegetable Soup

Yield:	4 servings
Prep Time:	15 minutes
Cook Time:	8 hours in slow cooker

Ingredients for Single Meal

- 1 lb. ground beef
- 15 oz. can black beans
- 15 oz. can diced tomatoes
- 3 cups frozen mixed vegetables
- 1 Tbsp Italian seasoning
- 1 Tbsp minced onion
- 1 tsp garlic powder
- 3 cups beef broth
- Salt and pepper
- Side: dinner rolls
- 1 gallon-size freezer baggie

Cooking Directions for Single Meal

1. Brown and drain the ground beef.
2. Add all the ingredients to the slow cooker, except the dinner rolls. Set slow cooker on low and cook for 8 hours.
3. Warm the dinner rolls, just before dinner.
4. Serve Slow Cooker Beef and Vegetable Soup with dinner rolls.

Freezeasy Meal Prep Directions

- Brown and drain the ground beef. Let cool before adding to freezer baggie.
- Open, drain and rinse 1 can of black beans.
- Open 1 can of diced tomatoes.
- To gallon-size plastic freezer baggie, add the following ingredients:
  - Browned ground beef
  - 15 oz. can black beans
  - 15 oz. can diced tomatoes
  - 3 cups frozen mixed vegetables
  - 1 Tbsp Italian seasoning
  - 1 Tbsp minced onion
  - 1 tsp garlic powder
  - 3 cups beef broth
  - Salt and pepper
- Remove as much air as possible and seal. Add label to baggie and freeze.

Freeze & Thaw Instructions

Put baggie in the freezer and freeze up to 6 months in fridge freezer or 12 months in a deep freezer. Thaw in the fridge overnight, or a warm bowl of water for about 20 minutes, before transferring to the slow cooker and cooking on low for 8 hours.

Slow Cooker Beef Stroganoff

Yield:	4 servings
Prep Time:	10 minutes
Cook Time:	8 hours in slow cooker

Ingredients for Single Meal

- 1 lb. ground beef
- 1 Tbsp minced onion
- 1 tsp garlic powder
- 1 cup beef broth
- 1 tsp paprika
- 10 oz. can cream of mushroom
- Salt and pepper
- 1 cup sour cream
- Side: egg noodles
- Side: veggies
- 1 gallon-size freezer baggie

Cooking Directions for Single Meal

1. In a large skillet, brown the ground beef with the minced onion and garlic powder. Add the browned ground beef into the base of the slow cooker.
2. Stir in 1 cup beef broth, then sprinkle the paprika and combine with the meat and broth. Pour the cream of mushroom soup over the top and sprinkle with salt and pepper.
3. Set the slow cooker on low and cook for 8 hours. Just before serving, stir in 1 cup sour cream into the beef mixture.
4. Cook the egg noodles, as directed.
5. Prepare veggies.
6. Serve Slow Cooker Beef Stroganoff over egg noodles with veggies.

Freezeasy Meal Prep Directions

- Brown the ground beef with 1 Tbsp minced onion and 1 tsp garlic powder. Drain and set aside to cool.
- Open 1 can of cream of mushroom soup.
- To gallon-size plastic freezer baggie, add the following ingredients:
  - Browned ground beef
  - 1 cup beef broth
  - 1 tsp paprika
  - Can of cream of mushroom soup
- Remove as much air as possible and seal. Add label to baggie and freeze.

Freeze & Thaw Instructions

Put baggie in the freezer and freeze up to 6 months in fridge freezer or 12 months in a deep freezer. Thaw in the fridge overnight, or a warm bowl of water for about 20 minutes, before transferring to the slow cooker and cooking on low for 8 hours. Just before serving, stir in 1 cup of sour cream as directed.

Slow Cooker Cheeseburger Chili

Yield: 4 servings
Prep Time: 15 minutes
Cook Time: 8 hours in slow cooker

Ingredients for Single Meal

- 1 lb. ground beef
- 1 Tbsp minced onion
- 1 tsp garlic powder
- 15 oz. can white beans
- 2 cups beef broth
- 2 cups shredded cheddar cheese
- 2 cups whole milk or heavy cream
- Salt and pepper
- Garnish: sour cream
- Side: veggies
- 1 gallon-size freezer baggie

Cooking Directions for Single Meal

1. In a skillet, brown the ground beef with minced onion and garlic powder. Drain.
2. To the slow cooker, add the browned ground beef, can white beans, and the beef broth. Set on low and cook for 8 hours.
3. Once done cooking, stir in half of shredded cheddar cheese and the whole milk or heavy cream to the chili in the slow cooker, and keep on warm until ready to serve.
4. Prepare veggies.
5. Serve Slow Cooker Cheeseburger Chili with bacon and shredded cheese garnish, and side of veggies.

Freezeasy Meal Prep Directions

- Brown the ground beef with 1 Tbsp minced onion and 1 tsp garlic powder. Drain and let cool before adding to bags.
- Open 1 can of white beans.
- To gallon-size plastic freezer baggie, add the following ingredients:
  - Browned ground beef
  - Can of white beans
- Do NOT add the beef broth to the freezer bag.
- Remove as much air as possible and seal. Add label to baggie and freeze.

Freeze & Thaw Instructions

Put baggie in the freezer and freeze up to 6 months in fridge freezer or 12 months in a deep freezer. Thaw in the fridge overnight, or a warm bowl of water for about 20 minutes, before transferring to the slow cooker, adding the beef broth, and cooking on low for 8 hours. Once finished cooking, stir in other ingredients as directed.

Slow Cooker Chili Mac

Yield: 4 servings
Prep Time: 15 minutes
Cook Time: 8 hours in slow cooker

Ingredients for Single Meal

- 1 lb. ground beef
- 1 Tbsp minced onion
- 1 tsp garlic powder
- 15 oz. can black beans
- 15 oz. can diced tomatoes
- 2 Tbsp chili powder
- 1 tsp ground cumin
- Salt and pepper
- 2 cups beef broth
- 16 oz. box elbow pasta noodles
- Garnish: shredded cheddar cheese
- Side: veggies
- 1 gallon-size freezer baggie

Cooking Directions for Single Meal

1. Brown the ground beef with minced onion and garlic powder. Drain well. Add the browned ground beef, black beans, diced tomatoes, chili powder, ground cumin and beef broth to the slow cooker. Set on low and cook for 8 hours.
2. With 1 hour left in slow cooker, add the pasta to the slow cooker with 1-2 cups hot water (depending on how much liquid is in the chili, see notes below) and let it cook the remainder of the slow cooking cycle.
3. Season with salt and pepper to taste.
4. Prepare veggies.
5. Serve Slow Cooker Chili Mac with shredded cheese garnish and side of veggies.

Freezeasy Meal Prep Directions

- Brown the ground beef, 1 Tbsp minced onion and 1 tsp garlic powder. Drain and let cool.
- Open 1 can of diced tomatoes.
- Open, drain and rinse 1 can of black beans.
- To gallon-size plastic freezer baggie, add the following ingredients:
  - Browned ground beef
  - Black beans
  - Diced tomatoes
  - 2 Tbsp chili powder
  - 1 tsp ground cumin
  - 2 cups beef broth
  - Salt and pepper
- Do not add pasta to freezer baggie.
- Remove as much air as possible and seal. Add label to baggie and freeze.

Freeze & Thaw Instructions

Put baggie in the freezer and freeze up to 6 months in fridge freezer or 12 months in a deep freezer. Thaw in the fridge overnight, or a warm bowl of water for about 20 minutes, before transferring to the slow cooker and cooking on low for 8 hours. IMPORTANT: When there is 1 hour left in the cooking cycle, add the pasta plus about 2 cups of hot water. You might need to add a little more liquid, depending on how much liquid is already in there and how "hot" your slow cooker runs. The pasta will soak in about 2 to 2 ½ cups of liquid.

Slow Cooker Cowboy Chili

Yield:	4 servings
Prep Time:	10 minutes
Cook Time:	8 hours in slow cooker

Ingredients for Single Meal

- 1 1/2 lbs. ground beef
- 1 small white onion
- 1 tsp minced garlic
- 15 oz. can red kidney beans
- 15 oz. can black beans
- 15 oz. can tomato sauce
- 1 cup red salsa
- 1 cup beef broth
- 1 Tbsp chili powder
- 1 tsp ground cumin
- Salt and pepper
- Garnish: shredded cheddar cheese
- Side: veggies
- Side: dinner rolls
- 1 gallon-size freezer baggie

Cooking Directions for Single Meal

1. Chop the small white onion.
2. Open the can of tomato sauce. Open, drain and rinse the cans of red kidney beans and black beans.
3. In a large skillet, brown the ground beef with the chopped onion and minced garlic. Drain, if needed.
4. To the slow cooker, add the browned ground beef with the red kidney beans, black beans, tomato sauce, salsa, beef broth, chili powder, and cumin. Stir it well and then set on low for 8 hours. Once cooked, season with salt and pepper to taste.
5. Prepare veggies.
6. Warm the dinner rolls.
7. Serve Slow Cooker Cowboy Chili with shredded cheese garnish, and side of veggies and dinner rolls.

Freezeasy Meal Prep Directions

- Chop 1 small white onion.
- Brown the ground beef with the chopped onion and 1 tsp minced garlic. Drain and let cool.
- Open, drain and rinse 1 can of red kidney beans and 1 can of black beans. Open 1 can of tomato sauce.
- To gallon-size plastic freezer baggie, add the following ingredients:
  - Browned ground beef
  - Chopped onion
  - 15 oz. can red kidney beans
  - 15 oz. can black beans
  - 15 oz. can tomato sauce
  - 1 cup red salsa
  - 1 cup beef broth
  - 1 Tbsp chili powder
  - 1 tsp ground cumin
- Remove as much air as possible and seal. Add label to baggie and freeze.

Freeze & Thaw Instructions

Put baggie in the freezer and freeze up to 6 months in fridge freezer or 12 months in a deep freezer. Thaw in the fridge overnight, or a warm bowl of water for about 20 minutes, before transferring all of the contents of the baggie into slow cooker insert. Set on low and cook for 8 hours.

Slow Cooker Creamy Taco Soup

Yield: 4 servings
Prep Time: 10 minutes
Cook Time: 8 hours in slow cooker

Ingredients for Single Meal

- 1 lb. ground beef
- 1 Tbsp minced onion
- 1 tsp garlic powder
- 1 green bell pepper
- 15 oz. can black beans
- 15 oz. can corn
- 2 - 15 oz. cans diced tomatoes
- 2 cups beef broth
- 2 packets taco seasoning
- 1 cup sour cream
- Garnish: crushed tortilla chips
- Garnish: shredded Mexican blend cheese
- Side: veggies
- 1 gallon-size freezer baggie

Cooking Directions for Single Meal

1. Brown the ground beef with the minced onion and garlic powder. Drain.
2. Seed and chop the green bell pepper.
3. Open, drain and rinse the black beans. Open and drain the can of corn.
4. To a 6 qt or larger slow cooker, add the browned ground beef, chopped bell pepper, drained and rinsed black beans, drained corn, 2 cans of diced tomatoes, and beef broth. Stir in the taco seasoning. Set on low and cook for 8 hours. Just before serving, swirl in the sour cream into the soup.
5. Prepare veggies.
6. Ladle soup into bowls. Top with crushed tortilla chips and cheese.
7. Serve Slow Cooker Creamy Taco Soup with veggies.

Freezeasy Meal Prep Directions

- Brown the ground beef with the minced onion and garlic powder. Drain and let cool.
- Seed and chop the green bell pepper.
- Open, drain and rinse 1 can of black beans. Open and drain 1 can of corn. Open 2 cans of diced tomatoes.
- To gallon-size plastic freezer baggie, add the following ingredients:
  - Browned ground beef
  - Chopped bell peppers
  - Can of black beans
  - Can of corn
  - Cans of diced tomatoes
  - Salt and pepper
  - Do NOT add the sour cream to the freezer bag
- Remove as much air as possible and seal. Add label to baggie and freeze.

Freeze & Thaw Instructions

Place baggie in the freezer and freeze up to 6 months in fridge freezer or 12 months in a deep freezer. Thaw in the fridge overnight, or a warm bowl of water for about 20 minutes, before transferring to the slow cooker, adding 2 cups of beef broth and taco seasoning and cooking on low for 8 hours. Swirl in the sour cream at the end of cooking cycle and just before serving.

Slow Cooker Layered Enchiladas

Yield: 4 servings
Prep Time: 10 minutes
Cook Time: 4 hours in slow cooker

Ingredients for Single Meal

- 1 lb. ground beef
- 1 Tbsp minced onion
- 1 tsp garlic powder
- 15 oz. can black beans
- 12 oz. can enchilada sauce
- 4 oz. can green chiles
- 1 cup red salsa
- 2 Tbsp chili powder
- 1 tsp ground cumin
- Salt and pepper
- 8 flour tortillas
- 2 cups shredded cheddar cheese
- Garnish: avocado
- Side: veggies
- 1 gallon-size freezer baggie

Cooking Directions for Single Meal

1. Open, drain, and rinse the black beans. Open the cans of enchilada sauce and green chilies.
2. In a large skillet, brown the ground beef with the minced onion and garlic powder. Drain and return to the stove. Stir in the black beans, enchilada sauce, green chilies, red salsa, chili powder, ground cumin and salt and pepper.
3. Spray the slow cooker insert with non-stick cooking spray. Add 1 or 2 flour tortillas on the bottom of the slow cooker insert. Spoon half of the ground beef mixture on top, then add a third of the cheese. Repeat the tortilla, ground beef, and cheese layers. Add 1 more layer of tortillas and the remaining cheese on top.
4. Set on low and cook for 4 hours.
5. Prepare the veggies.
6. Serve Slow Cooker Layered Enchiladas with avocado garnish and veggies.

Freezeasy Meal Prep Directions

- Brown 1 lb. ground beef with 1 Tbsp minced onion and 1 tsp garlic powder. Drain and let cool.
- Open, drain and rinse 1 can of black beans. Open 1 can of red enchilada sauce. Open 1 can of green chilies.
- To gallon-size plastic freezer baggie, add the following ingredients:
  - Browned ground beef
  - 15 oz. can black beans
  - 10 oz. can red enchilada sauce
  - 4 oz. can green chilies
  - 1 cup red salsa
  - 2 Tbsp chili powder
  - 1 tsp ground cumin
  - Salt and pepper
- Remove as much air as possible and seal. Add label to baggie and freeze.

Freeze & Thaw Instructions

Put baggie in the freezer and freeze up to 6 months in fridge freezer or 12 months in a deep freezer. Thaw in the fridge overnight, or a warm bowl of water for about 20 minutes, before layering the enchiladas into the slow cooker as directed.

Slow Cooker Sweet & Sour Meatballs

Yield: 4 servings
Prep Time: 10 minutes
Cook Time: 8 hours in slow cooker

Ingredients for Single Meal

- 1 lb. precooked frozen meatballs
- 1 small white onion
- 1 green bell pepper
- 1 red bell pepper
- 15 oz. can tomato sauce
- 3 Tbsp soy sauce
- 1/4 cup brown sugar
- 1/4 cup cider vinegar
- 20 oz. can pineapple chunks
- Salt and pepper
- 1 Tbsp cornstarch
- Side: rice
- 1 gallon-size freezer baggie

Cooking Directions for Single Meal

1. Dice onion. Seed and dice both peppers. Open and drain pineapple.
2. To the slow cooker, add the precooked meatballs, diced onion pieces, diced green and red bell pepper pieces.
3. In a small mixing bowl, whisk together the tomato sauce, soy sauce, brown sugar and cider vinegar. Pour over the meatballs and veggies. Add the pineapple chunks on top of the sauce. Add salt and pepper, to taste.
4. Set slow cooker on low and cook for 8 hours. With about 30 minutes left in the cooking cycle, whisk in the cornstarch to thicken the sauce around the beef and veggies.
5. TIP: In a small bowl, whisk together the 1 Tbsp cornstarch with 1 Tbsp of warm water then pour into the sauce. This will prevent the cornstarch from clumping in the sauce.
6. Prepare rice.
7. Serve Slow Cooker Sweet & Sour Meatballs over rice.

Freezeasy Meal Prep Directions

- Open 1 can of tomato sauce.
- Dice 1 green bell pepper and 1 red bell pepper.
- Dice 1 small white onion.
- Whisk together can tomato sauce, 3 Tbsp soy sauce, 1/4 cup brown sugar, and 1/4 cup cider vinegar.
- Open and drain 1 can of pineapple chunks.
- To gallon-size plastic freezer baggie, add the following ingredients:
  - 1 lb. frozen meatballs
  - Diced white onions
  - Diced green bell peppers
  - Diced red bell peppers
  - Prepared sweet n sour sauce
  - 20 oz. can pineapple chunks
  - Salt and pepper to taste
  - Note: Do not add cornstarch to the freezer bag.
- Remove as much air as possible and seal. Add label and freeze.

Freeze & Thaw Instructions

Put baggie in the freezer and freeze up to 6 months in fridge freezer or 12 months in a deep freezer. Thaw in the fridge overnight, or a warm bowl of water for about 20 minutes, before transferring to the slow cooker and cooking on low for 8 hours. With about 30 minutes left in the cooking cycle, whisk in the cornstarch to thicken the sauce around the beef and veggies.

Slow Cooker Taco Soup

Yield: 4 servings
Prep Time: 10 minutes
Cook Time: 8 hours in slow cooker

Ingredients for Single Meal

- 1 lb. ground beef
- 1 Tbsp minced onion
- 1 tsp garlic powder
- 1 green bell pepper
- 15 oz. can black beans
- 15 oz. can corn
- 2 - 15 oz. cans diced tomatoes
- 2 cups beef broth
- 2 packets taco seasoning
- Garnish: crushed tortilla chips
- Garnish: shredded Mexican blend cheese
- Side: veggies
- 1 gallon-size freezer baggie

Cooking Directions for Single Meal

1. Brown the ground beef with the minced onion and garlic powder. Drain.
2. Seed and chop the green bell pepper.
3. Open, drain and rinse the black beans. Open and drain the can of corn.
4. To a 6 qt or larger slow cooker, add the browned ground beef, chopped bell pepper, drained and rinsed black beans, drained corn, 2 cans of diced tomatoes, and beef broth. Stir in the taco seasoning. Set on low and cook for 8 hours.
5. Prepare veggies.
6. Ladle soup into bowls. Top with crushed tortilla chips and cheese.
7. Serve Slow Cooker Taco Soup with veggies.

Freezeasy Meal Prep Directions

- Brown the ground beef with 1 Tbsp minced onion and 1 tsp garlic powder. Drain and let cool.
- Seed and chop 1 green bell pepper.
- Open, drain and rinse 1 can of black beans. Open and drain 1 can of corn. Open 2 cans of diced tomatoes.
- To gallon-size plastic freezer baggie, add the following ingredients:
  ◦ Browned ground beef
  ◦ Chopped bell pepper
  ◦ Can of black beans
  ◦ Can of corn
  ◦ Cans of diced tomatoes
  ◦ Salt and pepper
  ◦ Do not add beef broth before freezing.
- Remove as much air as possible and seal. Add label to baggie and freeze.

Freeze & Thaw Instructions

Place baggie in the freezer and freeze up to 6 months in fridge freezer or 12 months in a deep freezer. Thaw in the fridge overnight, or a warm bowl of water for about 20 minutes, before transferring to the slow cooker, adding 2 cups of beef broth and taco seasoning and cooking on low for 8 hours.

Freezer to Slow Cooker Pork Chop Recipes

Slow Cooker Caesar Pork Chops and Potatoes

Slow Cooker Cheesy Garlic Pork Chops

Slow Cooker Creamy Ranch Pork Chops

Slow Cooker Dijon Pork Chops

Slow Cooker Ginger Peach Pork Chops

Slow Cooker Hawaiian Pork Chops

Slow Cooker Islander Pork Chops

Slow Cooker Marsala Pork Chops

Slow Cooker Sweet Chili Pork Chops

Slow Cooker Caesar Pork Chops and Potatoes

Yield:	4 servings
Prep Time:	5 minutes
Cook Time:	4 hours in slow cooker

Ingredients for Single Meal

- 4 boneless pork chops
- Salt and pepper
- 2 lb. bag fingerling potatoes
- 1 cup Caesar salad dressing
- 1 packet Italian seasoning
- Garnish: shredded Parmesan cheese
- Side: salad
- 1 gallon-size freezer baggie

Cooking Directions for Single Meal

1. Open the Italian seasoning packet and sprinkle into shallow dish or plate. Press both sides of the pork chops into the seasoning and then place into the the base of the slow cooker. Season with a little salt and pepper and then add the fingerling potatoes around the pork chops. Drizzle the Caesar dressing over the pork chops and potatoes.
2. If your slow cooker runs hot, add ½ to 1 cup of water to the base of the slow cooker to prevent pork chops from drying out.
3. Set the slow cooker on low and cook for 4 hours.
4. Prepare the salad.
5. Serve Slow Cooker Caesar Pork Chops and Potatoes with shredded Parmesan garnish and side salad.

Freezeasy Meal Prep Directions

- Open 1 Italian seasoning packet and sprinkle into shallow dish or plate. Press both sides of the pork chops into the seasoning.
- To gallon-size pwlastic freezer baggie, add the following ingredients:
  - 4 seasoned boneless pork chops
  - Salt and pepper
  - 2 lb. bag fingerling potatoes
  - 1 cup Caesar salad dressing
- Remove as much air as possible and seal. Add label to baggie and freeze.

Freeze & Thaw Instructions

Put baggie in the freezer and freeze up to 6 months in fridge freezer or 12 months in a deep freezer. Thaw in the fridge overnight, or a warm bowl of water for about 20 minutes, before transferring to the slow cooker and cooking on low for 4 hours.

Slow Cooker Cheesy Garlic Pork Chops

Yield: 4 servings
Prep Time: 5 minutes
Cook Time: 4 hours in slow cooker

Ingredients for Single Meal

- 4 boneless pork chops
- Salt and pepper
- 2 Tbsp melted butter
- 2 tsp minced garlic
- 1 tsp onion powder
- 1 cup shredded mild cheddar cheese
- Side: dinner rolls
- Side: veggies
- 1 gallon-size freezer baggie

Cooking Directions for Single Meal

1. Place the pork chops into the slow cooker insert and season with salt and pepper.
2. If your slow cooker runs hot, add ½ to 1 cup of water to the base of the slow cooker to prevent pork chops from drying out.
3. In a small bowl, stir the melted butter, minced garlic, and onion powder. Brush it onto the pork chops. Add a few pinchfuls of shredded mild cheddar cheese onto each pork chop.
4. Slow cook on low for 4 hours. Let rest for 5 minutes before serving or slicing. Cooking time may vary depending on thickness of the pork chops.
5. Prepare veggies.
6. Warm the dinner rolls.
7. Serve Slow Cooker Cheesy Garlic Pork Chops with veggies and dinner rolls.

Freezeasy Meal Prep Directions

- In a small bowl, stir 2 Tbsp melted butter, 2 tsp minced garlic, and 1 tsp onion powder.
- To each gallon size freezer baggie, add the following ingredients:
  ○ 4 boneless pork chops
  ○ Melted butter mixture, brushed onto each pork chop
- Remove as much air as possible, add label and freeze.

Freeze & Thaw Instructions

Put bag in the freezer and freeze up to 6 months in fridge freezer or 12 months in a deep freezer. Thaw in the fridge overnight, or a shallow dish of warm water for about 20 minutes, before transferring to the slow cooker, adding shredded cheese onto pork chops and cooking as directed.

Slow Cooker Creamy Ranch Pork Chops

Yield: 4 servings
Prep Time: 20 minutes
Cook Time: 8 hours in slow cooker

Ingredients for Single Meal

- 4 Tbsp butter
- 4 Tbsp all purpose flour
- 2 cups milk
- 1 tsp salt
- 1 tsp pepper
- 1 cup baby bella mushrooms
- 4 boneless pork chops
- 2 Tbsp ranch dressing mix
- 4 oz. cream cheese
- Side: veggies
- Side: dinner rolls
- 1 gallon-size freezer baggie

Cooking Directions for Single Meal

1. In a large skillet, make the homemade cream of mushroom soup. Melt 4 Tbsp butter and whisk in 4 Tbsp flour. Then quickly whisk in 2 cups milk, 1 tsp salt, pepper to taste. Bring to bubbling. Once thickened, add 1 cup chopped baby bella mushrooms. Let simmer 5 minutes.
2. Place the pork chops in the base of the slow cooker and season with salt and pepper and then add the ranch dressing mix spices over the top. Pour the homemade cream of mushroom soup over top of the pork chops.
3. Set your slow cooker on low and cook for 8 hours. When there is 30 minutes left in the cooking cycle, switch the slow cooker to high and add 4 oz. cubed cream cheese. Stir just before serving.
4. Serve Creamy Ranch Pork Chops with veggies and dinner rolls.

Freezeasy Meal Prep Directions

- Chop 1 cup baby bella mushrooms.
- In a large skillet, make the homemade cream of mushroom soup. Melt 4 Tbsp butter and whisk in 4 Tbsp flour. Then quickly whisk in 2 cups milk, 1 tsp salt, pepper to taste. Bring to bubbling. Once thickened, add chopped baby bella mushrooms. Let simmer 5 minutes. Then let cool before adding to baggie.
- To gallon-size plastic freezer baggie, add the following ingredients:
  - 4 boneless pork chops
  - Salt and pepper
  - Homemade cream of mushroom soup
  - 2 Tbsp ranch dressing mix
- Note: Do NOT add cream cheese at this time.
- Remove as much air as possible and seal. Add label to baggie and freeze.

Freeze & Thaw Instructions

Put baggie in the freezer and freeze up to 6 months in fridge freezer or 12 months in a deep freezer. Thaw in the fridge overnight, or a warm bowl of water for about 20 minutes, before transferring to the slow cooker and cooking on low for 8 hours. With 30 minutes left in the cooking cycle, switch to high and stir in 4 oz. cream cheese into the sauce, then let finish cooking.

Slow Cooker Dijon Pork Chops

Yield: 4 servings
Prep Time: 5 minutes
Cook Time: 8 hours in slow cooker

Ingredients for Single Meal

- 4 boneless pork chops
- 1 small white onion
- 10 oz. can cream of mushroom soup
- 2 Tbsp milk
- 1/4 cup Dijon mustard
- 1 tsp minced garlic
- 1/2 tsp pepper
- 1/2 tsp salt
- Side: mashed potatoes
- Side: salad
- 1 gallon-size freezer baggie

Cooking Directions for Single Meal

1. Slice the white onion into half-moons.
2. Place the pork chops into the base of the slow cooker.
3. In a small mixing bowl, combine the cream of mushroom soup, milk, Dijon mustard, garlic, salt and pepper. Pour over the pork chops in the slow cooker. Set the slow cooker on low and cook for 8 hours.
4. Prepare the mashed potatoes.
5. Prepare the salad.
6. Serve Slow Cooker Dijon Pork Chops with mashed potatoes and salad.

Freezeasy Meal Prep Directions

- Slice 1 small white onion into half-moons.
- Open 1 can of cream of mushroom soup.
- To gallon-size plastic freezer baggie, add the following ingredients:
  - 4 boneless pork chops
  - Sliced onions
  - 10 oz. can cream of mushroom soup
  - 2 Tbsp milk
  - 1/4 cup Dijon mustard
  - 1 tsp minced garlic
  - 1/2 tsp pepper
  - 1/2 tsp salt
- Remove as much air as possible and seal. Add label to baggie and freeze.

Freeze & Thaw Instructions

Put baggie in the freezer and freeze up to 6 months in fridge freezer or 12 months in a deep freezer. Thaw in the fridge overnight, or a warm bowl of water for about 20 minutes, before transferring to the slow cooker and cooking on low for 6 to 8 hours.

Slow Cooker Ginger Peach Pork Chops

Yield: 4 servings
Prep Time: 10 minutes
Cook Time: 8 hours in slow cooker

Ingredients for Single Meal

- 4 boneless pork chops
- Salt and pepper
- 1 cup peach preserves
- 1 Tbsp sesame oil
- 1 tsp ground ginger
- Side: veggies
- Side: mashed potatoes
- 1 gallon-size freezer baggie

Cooking Directions for Single Meal

1. Place the pork chops into the slow cooker insert and season with salt and pepper.
2. In a small bowl, mix together the peach preserves, sesame oil and ground ginger. Evenly divide and coat each pork chop.
3. If your slow cooker runs hot, add ½ to 1 cup of water to the base of the slow cooker to prevent pork chops from drying out.
4. Slow cook on low for 8 hours. Let rest for 5 minutes before serving or slicing. Cooking time may vary depending on thickness of the pork chops.
5. Prepare veggies.
6. Prepare mashed potatoes.
7. Serve Slow Cooker Ginger Peach Pork Chops with veggies and mashed potatoes.

Freezeasy Meal Prep Directions

- In a small bowl, mix together 1 cup peach preserves, 1 Tbsp sesame oil and 1 tsp ground ginger.
- To each gallon size freezer baggie, add the following ingredients:
  - 4 boneless pork chops
  - Salt and pepper
  - Peach preserve mixture, onto each of the pork chops
- Remove as much air from bag as possible, add label and freeze.

Freeze & Thaw Instructions

Put baggie in the freezer and freeze up to 6 months in fridge freezer or 12 months in a deep freezer. Thaw in the fridge overnight, or a warm shallow dish of water for about 20 minutes, before transferring to the slow cooker and cooking as directed.

Slow Cooker Hawaiian Pork Chops

Yield: 4 servings
Prep Time: 10 minutes
Cook Time: 8 hours in slow cooker

Ingredients for Single Meal

- 4 boneless pork chops
- Salt and pepper
- 1/2 cup soy sauce
- 8 oz. can tomato sauce
- 20 oz. can pineapple slices
- 1/2 cup brown sugar
- 2 tsp minced garlic
- 1 Tbsp cornstarch
- Side: dinner rolls
- Side: salad
- 1 gallon-size freezer baggie

Cooking Directions for Single Meal

1. To the slow cooker, add the pork chops and sprinkle with salt and pepper.
2. In a small mixing bowl, whisk together the soy sauce, tomato sauce, brown sugar and minced garlic with 1/4 cup of pineapple juice from the can. Pour over the pork chops in the slow cooker. Place the pineapple slices around and on top of the pork chops. Discard the remaining pineapple juice.
3. Set slow cooker on low and cook for 8 hours. With 30 minutes left in the cooking cycle, whisk in the cornstarch to thicken the sauce.
4. TIP: In a small bowl, whisk together the 1 Tbsp cornstarch with 1 Tbsp of warm water then pour into the sauce. This will prevent the cornstarch from clumping in the sauce.
5. Prepare salad. Warm dinner rolls.
6. Serve Slow Cooker Hawaiian Pork Chops with rolls and salad.

Freezeasy Meal Prep Directions

- Open 1 can of tomato sauce.
- Open and drain juice from 1 can of pineapple slices. Reserve 1/4 cup pineapple juice.
- In a small mixing bowl, whisk together 1/2 cup soy sauce, 1 can tomato sauce, 1/2 cup brown sugar and 2 tsp minced garlic with 1/4 cup of pineapple juice from the can. Do not whisk in cornstarch now.
- To gallon-size plastic freezer baggie, add the following ingredients in the order listed:
  - 4 boneless pork chops
  - Salt and pepper
  - Prepared sauce
  - Can of pineapple slices
- Remove as much as air as possible and seal.

Freeze & Thaw Instructions

Put baggie in the freezer and freeze up to 6 months in fridge freezer or 12 months in a deep freezer. Thaw in the fridge overnight, or a warm bowl of water for about 20 minutes, before transferring to the slow cooker and cooking on low for 8 hours.

Slow Cooker Islander Pork Chops

Yield:	4 servings
Prep Time:	10 minutes
Cook Time:	8 hours in slow cooker

Ingredients for Single Meal

- 4 boneless pork chops
- Salt and pepper
- 1 red bell pepper
- 1/2 small white onion
- 2 Tbsp brown sugar
- 1 Tbsp Jerk or Caribbean spice blend
- 20 oz. can pineapple chunks
- Side: dinner rolls or rice
- Side: veggies
- 1 gallon-size freezer baggie

Cooking Directions for Single Meal

1. To the slow cooker, add the pork chops and sprinkle with salt and pepper.
2. In a small mixing bowl, toss together the chopped bell pepper, chopped onion, brown sugar and Jerk or Caribbean spice seasoning. Stir in the pineapple chunks and juices from the can. Pour over the pork chops in the slow cooker.
3. Set slow cooker on low and cook for 8 hours.
4. Serve Slow Cooker Islander Pork Chops with side dishes.

Freezeasy Meal Prep Directions

- Chop 1/2 white onion.
- Seed and dice 1 red bell pepper.
- Open 1 can of pineapple chunks.
- To gallon-size plastic freezer baggie, add the following ingredients:
  - 4 boneless pork chops
  - Salt and pepper
  - Diced bell pepper
  - Chopped onion
  - 2 Tbsp brown sugar
  - 1 Tbsp Jerk or Caribbean spice seasoning
  - Can of pineapple chunks with juices
- Remove as much air as possible and seal. Add label to baggie and freeze.

Freeze & Thaw Instructions

Put baggie in the freezer and freeze up to 6 months in fridge freezer or 12 months in a deep freezer. Thaw in the fridge overnight, or a warm bowl of water for about 20 minutes, before transferring to the slow cooker and cooking on low for 8 hours.

Slow Cooker Marsala Pork Chops

Yield:	4 servings
Prep Time:	5 minutes
Cook Time:	8 hours in slow cooker

Ingredients for Single Meal

- 4 boneless pork chops
- 1 small white onion
- 2 tsp minced garlic
- 8 oz. sliced white mushrooms
- 1/2 cup marsala cooking wine
- 10 oz. can cream of mushroom soup
- Side: dinner rolls
- Side: salad
- 1 gallon-size freezer baggie

Cooking Directions for Single Meal

1. Slice the white onion.
2. Place the pork chops into the base of the slow cooker and add the sliced onions, minced garlic and sliced mushrooms over the top. Pour the marsala wine around the edges of the slow cooker insert. Spoon and spread the cream of mushroom soup over the top.
3. Set the slow cooker on low and cook for 8 hours.
4. Warm the dinner rolls.
5. Prepare the salad.
6. Serve Slow Cooker Marsala Pork Chops with dinner rolls and salad.

Freezeasy Meal Prep Directions

- Slice 1 small white onion.
- To gallon-size plastic freezer baggie, add the following ingredients:
  - 4 boneless pork chops
  - Sliced onion
  - 2 tsp minced garlic
  - 8 oz sliced mushrooms
  - 1/2 cup marsala cooking wine
  - 10 oz. can cream of mushroom soup
- Remove as much air as possible and seal. Add label to baggie and freeze.

Freeze & Thaw Instructions

Put baggie in the freezer and freeze up to 6 months in fridge freezer or 12 months in a deep freezer. Thaw in the fridge overnight, or a warm bowl of water for about 20 minutes, before transferring to the slow cooker and cooking on low for 8 hours.

Slow Cooker Sweet Chili Pork Chops

Yield:	4 servings
Prep Time:	5 minutes
Cook Time:	8 hours in slow cooker

Ingredients for Single Meal

- 4 boneless pork chops
- Salt and pepper
- 1/4 cup sweet Thai chili sauce
- Side: rice
- Side: veggies
- 1 gallon-size freezer baggie

Cooking Directions for Single Meal

1. Add the pork chops to the base of the slow cooker and season with salt and pepper. Brush the sweet Thai chili sauce onto each pork chop.
2. If your slow cooker runs hot, add ½ to 1 cup of water to the base of the slow cooker to prevent pork chops from drying out.
3. Set slow cooker on low and cook for 8 hours.
4. Cook the rice, as directed.
5. Prepare veggies.
6. Serve Slow Cooker Sweet Chili Pork Chops with veggies and rice.

Freezeasy Meal Prep Directions

- To each gallon size freezer baggie, add the following ingredients:
  - 4 boneless pork chops
  - Salt and pepper
  - Sweet Thai chili sauce, brushed onto the pork chops
- Remove as much air as possible, add label and freeze.

Freeze & Thaw Instructions

Put baggie in the freezer and freeze up to 6 months in fridge freezer or 12 months in a deep freezer. Thaw in the fridge overnight, or a shallow dish of warm water for about 20 minutes, before transferring to the slow cooker and cooking as directed. Add water, if necessary.

Freezer to Slow Cooker Pork Roast Recipes

Slow Cooker Adobo Pulled Pork Sandwiches
Slow Cooker Bacon Wrapped Pork Tenderloin
Slow Cooker Caribbean Pork Sliders
Slow Cooker Cranberry-Mustard Pork Roast
Slow Cooker Garlic-Orange Pork Tenderloin
Slow Cooker Jerk Pulled Pork Sliders
Slow Cooker North Carolina Pulled Pork
Slow Cooker Peach Glazed Pork Roast
Slow Cooker Pulled Pork Ragu
Slow Cooker Root Beer Pulled Pork
Slow Cooker Salsa Verde Pork Tacos
Slow Cooker Sweet 'n Spicy Shredded Pork Tacos
Slow Cooker Teriyaki Pork Tenderloin

Slow Cooker Adobo Pulled Pork Sandwiches

Yield: 4 servings
Prep Time: 10 minutes
Cook Time: 8 hours in slow cooker

Ingredients for Single Meal

- 2 lb. pork roast
- Salt and pepper
- 8 oz. can tomato sauce
- 2 Tbsp brown sugar
- 1 tsp garlic powder
- 1 tsp chili powder
- 1 Tbsp Adobo seasoning
- 8 hamburger buns
- Side: veggies
- Side: potato chips
- 1 gallon-size freezer baggie

Cooking Directions for Single Meal

1. Place the pork roast into the base of the slow cooker and season with salt and pepper.
2. In a small bowl, combine the tomato sauce, brown sugar, garlic powder, chili powder and Adobo seasoning. Pour over the pork roast. Add 1 cup water to the base of your slow cooker.
3. Set the slow cooker on low and cook for 8 hours. Once finished cooking, shred the pork roast with 2 forks and mix into the sauce.
4. Spoon the shredded pork onto buns.
5. Prepare the veggies.
6. Serve Adobo Pulled Pork Sandwiches with veggies and chips.

Freezeasy Meal Prep Directions

- Open 1 can of tomato sauce.
- In a small bowl, combine the can of tomato sauce, 2 Tbsp brown sugar, 1 tsp garlic powder, 1 tsp chili powder and 1 Tbsp Adobo seasoning.
- To gallon-size plastic freezer baggie, add the following ingredients:
  - 2 lb. pork roast
  - Salt and pepper
  - Prepared Adobo sauce
- Remove as much air as possible and seal. Add label to baggie and freeze.

Freeze & Thaw Instructions

Put baggie in the freezer and freeze up to 6 months in fridge freezer or 12 months in a deep freezer. Thaw in the fridge overnight, or a warm bowl of water for about 20 minutes, before transferring contents with 1 cup water to the slow cooker and cooking on low for 8 hours. Once finished cooking, shred the pork roast with 2 forks and mix into the sauce.

Slow Cooker Bacon Wrapped Pork Tenderloin

Yield: 4 servings
Prep Time: 10 minutes
Cook Time: 8 hours in slow cooker

Ingredients for Single Meal

- 2 lb. pork tenderloin
- 2 Tbsp brown sugar
- 2 tsp minced garlic
- 1 tsp salt
- 4 slices bacon
- Side: salad
- Side: mashed potatoes
- 1 gallon-size freezer baggie

Cooking Directions for Single Meal

1. In a small bowl, mix the brown sugar, minced garlic and salt. Press this mixture onto the top of the pork tenderloin. Wrap the pork tenderloin in the bacon slices, either wrapped all the way around, or criss-crossed and laid on top of the pork tenderloin.
2. Carefully place into the slow cooker and set the slow cooker on low and cook for 4 hours. If cooking from partially frozen, cook for 8 hours on low.
3. If needed, turn on the broiler on high and place the pork tenderloin and bacon underneath for 1-2 minutes to 'crisp up' the bacon slices.
4. Prepare the mashed potatoes.
5. Prepare the salad.
6. Serve Slow Cooker Bacon Wrapped Pork Tenderloin with salad and mashed potatoes.

Freezeasy Meal Prep Directions

- In a small bowl, mix 2 Tbsp brown sugar, 2 tsp minced garlic and 1 tsp salt.
- To gallon-size plastic freezer baggie, add the following ingredients:
  - 2 lb. pork tenderloin
  - Prepared rub
  - 4 slices bacon, wrapped around the tenderloin
- Remove as much air as possible and seal. Add label to baggie and freeze.

Freeze & Thaw Instructions

Put baggie in the freezer and freeze up to 6 months in fridge freezer or 12 months in a deep freezer. Thaw in the fridge overnight, or a warm bowl of water for about 20 minutes, before transferring to the slow cooker and cooking as directed.

Slow Cooker Caribbean Pork Sliders

Yield:	4 servings
Prep Time:	10 minutes
Cook Time:	8 hours in slow cooker

Ingredients for Single Meal

- 2 lb. pork roast
- Salt and pepper
- 1 Tbsp minced onion
- 1 tsp garlic powder
- 1 tsp ground cumin
- 1 tsp chipotle chili powder
- 1 cup BBQ sauce
- 12 slider buns
- Garnish: coleslaw
- Side: fruit
- 1 gallon-size freezer baggie

Cooking Directions for Single Meal

1. Place the pork roast into the base of the slow cooker. Season with salt and pepper, the minced onion, garlic powder, ground cumin and chipotle chili powder. Add the BBQ sauce over top. Pour 1 cup hot water around the pork into the base of the slow cooker.
2. Set on low and cook for 8 hours. Once cooked, shred with 2 forks and place the shredded pork onto slider buns with coleslaw.
3. Prepare fruit.
4. Serve Caribbean Pork Sliders with fruit.

Freezeasy Meal Prep Directions

- To gallon-size plastic freezer baggie, add the following ingredients:
  - 2 lb. pork roast
  - Salt and pepper
  - 1 Tbsp minced onion
  - 1 tsp garlic powder
  - 1 tsp ground cumin
  - 1 tsp chipotle chili powder
  - 1 cup BBQ sauce
- Remove as much air as possible and seal. Add label to baggie and freeze.

Freeze & Thaw Instructions

Put baggie in the freezer and freeze up to 6 months in fridge freezer or 12 months in a deep freezer. Thaw in the fridge overnight, or a warm bowl of water for about 20 minutes, before transferring to slow cooker. Add 1 cup of hot water and cook on low for 8 hours. Once cooked, shred with 2 forks and place the shredded pork onto slider buns with coleslaw.

Slow Cooker Cranberry-Mustard Pork Roast

Yield:	4 servings
Prep Time:	10 minutes
Cook Time:	8 hours in slow cooker

Ingredients for Single Meal

- 2 lb. pork roast
- Salt and pepper
- 1 tsp cinnamon
- 15 oz. can whole cranberries
- 1/4 cup spicy mustard
- Side: mashed potatoes
- Side: veggies
- 1 gallon-size freezer baggie

Cooking Directions for Single Meal

1. Place the pork roast into the base of the slow cooker insert. Season with salt, pepper and cinnamon.
2. If your slow cooker runs hot, add ½ to 1 cup of water to the base of the slow cooker to prevent pork roast from drying out.
3. In a small mixing bowl, combine the whole cranberries with the spicy mustard. Pour the sauce over top of the pork roast and set on low and cook for 8 hours.
4. Prepare the mashed potatoes and veggies.
5. Serve Slow Cooker Cranberry-Mustard Pork Roast with a side of mashed potatoes and veggies.

Freezeasy Meal Prep Directions

- Open the can of whole cranberries.
- Whisk together can whole cranberries sauce & 1/4 cup spicy mustard.
- To gallon-size plastic freezer baggie, add the following ingredients:
  - 2 lb. pork roast
  - Pinch of salt and pepper and dashes of cinnamon onto the pork roast
  - Prepared cranberry-mustard sauce
- Remove as much air as possible and seal. Add label to baggie and freeze.

Freeze & Thaw Instructions

Put baggie in the freezer and freeze up to 6 months in fridge freezer or 12 months in a deep freezer. Thaw in the fridge overnight, or a warm bowl of water for about 20 minutes, before transferring to the slow cooker and cooking on low for 8 hours.

Slow Cooker Garlic-Orange Pork Tenderloin

Yield: 4 servings
Prep Time: 5 minutes
Cook Time: 8 hours in slow cooker

Ingredients for Single Meal

- 2 lb. pork tenderloin
- Salt and pepper
- 1 cup orange juice
- 2 tsp minced garlic
- 1 tsp ground ginger
- 1 tsp dried thyme
- Side: mashed potatoes
- Side: veggies
- 1 gallon-size freezer baggie

Cooking Directions for Single Meal

1. Place the pork tenderloin into the base of the slow cooker and season with salt and pepper. Pour the orange juice on and around the pork and then add the minced garlic, ground ginger and dried thyme over the top.
2. Set the slow cooker on low and cook for 8 hours. Remove from slow cooker and let rest for 5 to 10 minutes before slicing.
3. Prepare the mashed potatoes.
4. Prepare veggies.
5. Serve Slow Cooker Garlic-Orange Pork Tenderloin with mashed potatoes and veggies.

Freezeasy Meal Prep Directions

- To gallon-size plastic freezer baggie, add the following ingredients:
  - 2 lb. pork tenderloin
  - Salt and pepper
  - 1 cup orange juice
  - 2 tsp minced garlic
  - 1 tsp ground ginger
  - 1 tsp dried thyme
- Remove as much air as possible and seal. Add label to baggie and freeze.

Freeze & Thaw Instructions

Put baggie in the freezer and freeze up to 6 months in fridge freezer or 12 months in a deep freezer. Thaw in the fridge overnight, or a warm bowl of water for about 20 minutes, before transferring to the slow cooker and cooking on low for 8 hours.

Slow Cooker Jerk Pulled Pork Sliders

Yield:	4 servings
Prep Time:	5 minutes
Cook Time:	8 hours in slow cooker

Ingredients for Single Meal

- 2 lb. pork roast
- Salt and pepper
- 1/4 cup lime juice
- 3 Tbsp Jerk seasoning
- 1 tsp garlic powder
- 1 tsp onion powder
- 1 tsp ground cumin
- 1 tsp brown sugar
- 8 oz. can sliced pineapple
- 12 slider buns
- Garnish: sliced green onions
- Side: fruit
- Side: chips
- 1 gallon-size freezer baggie

Cooking Directions for Single Meal

1. Place the pork roast into the base of the slow cooker and season with salt and pepper. Pour the lime juice on and around the pork. Season with the Jerk seasoning, garlic powder, onion powder, ground cumin and brown sugar. Place the pineapple slices over the top.
2. Set the slow cooker on low and cook for 8 hours. Once finished cooking, shred the pork with 2 forks and mix into the sauce. Strain before adding the pork to the sliders.
3. Assemble sliders by adding the shredded pork and sliced green onion garnish.
4. Prepare fruit.
5. Serve Slow Cooker Jerk Pulled Pork Sliders with fruit and chips.

Freezeasy Meal Prep Directions

- Open and drain 1 can of sliced pineapple.
- To gallon-size plastic freezer baggie, add the following ingredients:
  - 2 lb. pork roast
  - Salt and pepper
  - 1/4 cup lime juice
  - 3 Tbsp Jerk seasoning
  - 1 tsp garlic powder
  - 1 tsp onion powder
  - 1 tsp ground cumin
  - 1 tsp brown sugar
  - 8 oz. can sliced pineapple
- Remove as much air as possible and seal. Add label to baggie and freeze.

Freeze & Thaw Instructions

Put baggie in the freezer and freeze up to 6 months in fridge freezer or 12 months in a deep freezer. Thaw in the fridge overnight, or a warm bowl of water for about 20 minutes, before transferring to the slow cooker and cooking on low for 8 hours. Once finished cooking, shred the pork with 2 forks and mix into the sauce. Strain before adding the pork to the sliders.

Slow Cooker North Carolina Pulled Pork

Yield: 4 servings
Prep Time: 5 minutes
Cook Time: 8 hours in slow cooker

Ingredients for Single Meal

- 2 lb. pork roast
- Salt and pepper
- 2 cups BBQ sauce
- 1 tsp vinegar
- 1 tsp garlic powder
- 1 tsp onion powder
- 1 bag Coleslaw mix
- 4 hamburger buns
- Side: fruit
- Side: chips
- 1 gallon-size freezer baggie

Cooking Directions for Single Meal

1. Place the pork roast into the base of the slow cooker and season with salt and pepper. Pour the BBQ sauce and vinegar on and around the pork and season with the garlic powder and onion powder.
2. Set the slow cooker on low and cook for 8 hours. Once finished cooking, shred the pork with 2 forks and mix into the BBQ sauce. Strain before adding the pork to the sandwiches.
3. Prepare the Coleslaw mix as directed.
4. Assemble sandwiches by adding the shredded pork and Coleslaw to the hamburger buns.
5. Prepare fruit.
6. Serve Slow Cooker North Carolina Pulled Pork Sandwiches with fruit and chips.

Freezeasy Meal Prep Directions

- To gallon-size plastic freezer baggie, add the following ingredients:
  - 2 lb. pork roast
  - Salt and pepper
  - 2 cups BBQ sauce
  - 1 tsp vinegar
  - 1 tsp garlic powder
  - 1 tsp onion powder
- Remove as much air as possible and seal. Add label to baggie and freeze.

Freeze & Thaw Instructions

Put baggie in the freezer and freeze up to 6 months in fridge freezer or 12 months in a deep freezer. Thaw in the fridge overnight, or a warm bowl of water for about 20 minutes, before transferring to the slow cooker and cooking on low for 8 hours. Once finished cooking, shred the pork with 2 forks and mix into the BBQ sauce. Strain before adding the pork to the sandwiches.

Slow Cooker Peach Glazed Pork Roast

Yield: 4 servings
Prep Time: 5 minutes
Cook Time: 8 hours in slow cooker

Ingredients for Single Meal

- 2 lb. pork roast
- 1 tsp minced onion
- Salt and pepper
- 1/2 jar peach preserves
- 1 tsp ground ginger
- Side: rice
- Side: veggies
- 1 gallon-size freezer baggie

Cooking Directions for Single Meal

1. Place the roast in the base of the slow cooker and season with minced onion, salt and pepper. Add about 1/2 cup of water around the roast to keep the inside of the slow cooker humid and moist.
2. In a small bowl, whisk together the peach preserves and ginger. Spread directly over top of the pork roast. Set the slow cooker on low and cook for 8 hours. Once cooked, slice the pork.
3. Cook rice, as directed.
4. Prepare veggies.
5. Serve Slow Cooker Peach Glazed Pork Roast with rice and veggies.

Freezeasy Meal Prep Directions

- Whisk together about 1/2 jar peach preserves and 1 tsp ginger.
- To gallon-size plastic freezer baggie, add the following ingredients:
  - 2 lb. pork roast
  - 1 tsp minced onion
  - Salt and pepper
  - Prepared peach-ginger glaze
- Remove as much as air as possible and seal.

Freeze & Thaw Instructions

Put baggie in the freezer and freeze up to 6 months in fridge freezer or 12 months in a deep freezer. Thaw in the fridge overnight, or a warm bowl of water for about 20 minutes, before transferring to the slow cooker and cooking on low for 8 hours.

Slow Cooker Pulled Pork Ragu

Yield:	4 servings
Prep Time:	10 minutes
Cook Time:	8 hours in slow cooker

Ingredients for Single Meal

- 2 lb. pork tenderloin
- Salt and pepper
- 28 oz. can crushed tomatoes
- 7 oz. jar red peppers
- 3 tsp minced garlic
- 2 Tbsp Italian seasoning
- Side: pasta
- Side: salad
- 1 gallon-size freezer baggie

Cooking Directions for Single Meal

1. Open the can of crushed tomatoes. Drain the jar of roasted red peppers.
2. Place the pork tenderloin into the base of the slow cooker and season with salt and pepper. Pour the crushed tomatoes, drained roasted red peppers, minced garlic and Italian seasoning over the pork tenderloin.
3. Set the slow cooker on low and cook for 8 hours. Once finished cooking, shred the pork with 2 forks and mix into the ragu sauce.
4. Cook the pasta as directed.
5. Prepare the salad.
6. Serve Slow Cooker Pulled Pork Ragu over pasta with salad.

Freezeasy Meal Prep Directions

- Open 1 can of crushed tomatoes.
- Open and drain 1 jar of roasted red peppers.
- To gallon-size plastic freezer baggie, add the following ingredients:
  - 2 lb. pork tenderloin
  - Salt and pepper
  - 28 oz. can crushed tomatoes
  - 7 oz. jar roasted red peppers
  - 3 tsp minced garlic
  - 2 Tbsp Italian seasoning
- Remove as much air as possible and seal. Add label to baggie and freeze.

Freeze & Thaw Instructions

Put baggie in the freezer and freeze up to 6 months in fridge freezer or 12 months in a deep freezer. Thaw in the fridge overnight, or a warm bowl of water for about 20 minutes, before transferring to the slow cooker and cooking on low for 8 hours. Once finished cooking, shred the pork with 2 forks and mix into the ragu sauce.

Slow Cooker Root Beer Pulled Pork

Yield: 4 servings
Prep Time: 10 minutes
Cook Time: 8 hours in slow cooker

Ingredients for Single Meal

- 2 lb. pork roast
- 1/2 small red onion
- Salt and pepper
- 12 oz. can root beer
- 16 oz. bottle BBQ sauce
- 8 hamburger buns
- Side: Coleslaw salad kit
- Side: chips
- 1 gallon-size freezer baggie

Cooking Directions for Single Meal

1. Thinly slice the red onion.
2. Place the pork roast and red onion slices in the base of the slow cooker and sprinkle with salt and pepper. Pour the root beer and BBQ sauce over the pork roast. Set the slow cooker on low and cook for 8 hours. Once the pork roast is cooked, shred the meat with 2 forks and toss with the sauce.
3. Prepare the Coleslaw salad just before serving.
4. Spoon shredded pork onto hamburger buns and top with Coleslaw.
5. Serve Slow Cooker Root Beer Pulled Pork with chips.

Freezeasy Meal Prep Directions

- Thinly slice 1/2 small red onion.
- To gallon-size plastic freezer baggie, add the following ingredients:
  - 2 lbs pork roast
  - Red onion slices
  - Salt and pepper
  - 12 oz. can root beer
  - 16 oz. bottle BBQ sauce
- Remove as much air as possible and seal. Add label to baggie and freeze.

Freeze & Thaw Instructions

Put baggie in the freezer and freeze up to 6 months in fridge freezer or 12 months in a deep freezer. Thaw in the fridge overnight, or a warm bowl of water for about 20 minutes, before transferring to the slow cooker and cooking on low for 8 hours. Once the pork roast is cooked, shred the meat with 2 forks and toss with the sauce.

Slow Cooker Salsa Verde Pork Tacos

Yield:	4 servings
Prep Time:	10 minutes
Cook Time:	8 hours in slow cooker

Ingredients for Single Meal

- 2 lb. pork shoulder roast
- 1 tsp garlic powder
- 1 tsp ground cumin
- Salt and pepper
- 1 1/2 cups salsa verde sauce
- 1 large jalapeño
- 12 corn tortillas
- Garnish: crumbled goat cheese
- Garnish: sour cream
- Topping: jalapeño
- Topping: cilantro or avocado chunks
- Side: veggies
- 1 gallon-size freezer baggie

Cooking Directions for Single Meal

1. Place the pork roast into the base of the slow cooker and sprinkle the garlic powder, ground cumin, salt and pepper on top of the pork roast. Pour the salsa verde and add the diced jalapeños on top.
2. Set the slow cooker on low and cook for 8 hours. Once the cooking time is complete, shred the pork with 2 forks and remove from the slow cooker with slotted spoon when ready to serve.
3. Spoon the shredded pork into the corn tortillas and add preferred toppings.
4. Prepare veggies.
5. Serve Salsa Verde Shredded Pork Tacos with veggies and preferred toppings.

Freezeasy Meal Prep Directions

- Remove the seeds and dice 1 jalapeño.
- To gallon-size plastic freezer baggie, add the following ingredients:
  - 2 lb. pork shoulder roast
  - 1 tsp garlic powder
  - 1 tsp ground cumin
  - Salt and pepper
  - 1 1/2 cups salsa verde sauce
  - Diced jalapeño
- Remove as much air as possible and seal. Add label to baggie and freeze.

Freeze & Thaw Instructions

Put baggie in the freezer and freeze up to 6 months in fridge freezer or 12 months in a deep freezer. Thaw in a warm bowl of water for about 20 minutes, before transferring to the slow cooker and cooking on low for 8 hours. Once the cooking time is complete, shred the pork with 2 forks and remove from the slow cooker with slotted spoon when ready to serve.

Slow Cooker Sweet 'n Spicy Shredded Pork Tacos

Yield:	4 servings
Prep Time:	10 minutes
Cook Time:	8 hours in slow cooker

Ingredients for Single Meal

- 2 lb. pork roast
- 1 small white onion
- 1/2 cup brown sugar
- 3 tsp minced garlic
- 1 Tbsp ground cumin
- 1 tsp cayenne pepper
- 1 cup chicken stock
- 12 corn tortillas
- Garnish: lime wedges
- Garnish: pico de gallo
- Side: salad
- 1 gallon-size freezer baggie

Cooking Directions for Single Meal

1. Chop the white onion.
2. Place the pork roast into the base of the slow cooker and sprinkle the chopped onions around it. Sprinkle in the brown sugar, minced garlic, ground cumin, and cayenne pepper. Pour the chicken stock around the edges of the slow cooker. (Note: You could use water instead of chicken stock.)
3. Set the slow cooker on low and cook for 8 hours. Once finished cooking, shred the pork roast with 2 forks and mix into the sauce.
4. Spoon the shredded pork into corn tortillas and make tacos. Top with lime and pico de gallo.
5. Prepare the salad.
6. Serve Slow Cooker Sweet 'n Spicy Shredded Pork Tacos with salad.

Freezeasy Meal Prep Directions

- Chop 1 small white onion.
- To gallon-size plastic freezer baggie, add the following ingredients:
  - 2 lb. pork roast
  - Chopped white onion
  - 1/2 cup brown sugar
  - 3 tsp minced garlic
  - 1 Tbsp ground cumin
  - 1 tsp cayenne pepper
  - 1 cup chicken stock
- Remove as much air as possible and seal. Add label to baggie and freeze.

Freeze & Thaw Instructions

Put baggie in the freezer and freeze up to 6 months in fridge freezer or 12 months in a deep freezer. Thaw in the fridge overnight, or a bowl of warm water for about 20 minutes, before transferring to the slow cooker and cooking on low for 8 hours. Once finished cooking, shred the pork roast with 2 forks and mix into the sauce.

Slow Cooker Teriyaki Pork Tenderloin

Yield: 4 servings
Prep Time: 10 minutes
Cook Time: 8 hours in slow cooker

Ingredients for Single Meal

- 2 lb. pork tenderloin
- 1 small white onion
- 1 cup teriyaki sauce
- 2 tsp minced garlic
- 1 tsp crushed red pepper flakes
- Salt and pepper
- Garnish: sliced green onions
- Side: rice
- Side: veggies
- 1 gallon-size freezer baggie

Cooking Directions for Single Meal

1. Thinly slice the onion.
2. Add the pork tenderloin to the base of the slow cooker. Add the thin onion slices on top. Pour the teriyaki sauce onto the pork tenderloin and onion slices. Add the minced garlic and crushed red pepper flakes over the top. Sprinkle salt and pepper to taste.
3. Set on low and cook for 8 hours. Remove tenderloin from the slow cooker and let sit for 5 minutes before slicing. Spoon sauce out of slow cooker to serve over sliced pork pieces.
4. Cook the rice, as directed.
5. Prepare veggies.
6. Serve Teriyaki Pork Tenderloin with sliced green onions garnish, rice and veggies.

Freezeasy Meal Prep Directions

- Thinly slice 1 onion.
- To gallon-size plastic freezer baggie, add the following ingredients:
  ◦ 2 lb. pork tenderloin
  ◦ Sliced white onions
  ◦ 1 cup teriyaki sauce
  ◦ 2 tsp minced garlic
  ◦ 1 tsp crushed red pepper flakes
  ◦ Salt and pepper
- Remove as much air as possible and seal. Add label to baggie and freeze.

Freeze & Thaw Instructions

Put baggie in the freezer and freeze up to 6 months in fridge freezer or 12 months in a deep freezer. Thaw in the fridge overnight, or a warm bowl of water for about 20 minutes, before transferring to the slow cooker and cooking on low for 8 hours.

Freezer to Slow Cooker Seafood Recipes

Slow Cooker BBQ Shrimp

Slow Cooker Lemon & Dill Salmon

Slow Cooker Red Curry with Cod

Slow Cooker Sesame Salmon

Slow Cooker BBQ Shrimp

Yield:	4 servings
Prep Time:	10 minutes
Cook Time:	1 hour in slow cooker

Ingredients for Single Meal

- 2 lbs. peeled deveined shrimp
- 3 Tbsp butter
- 3 Tbsp Worcestershire sauce
- 2 tsp minced garlic
- 1 cup BBQ sauce
- Salt and pepper
- Garnish: lemon wedges
- Side: French loaf bread
- Side: veggies
- 1 gallon-size freezer baggie

Cooking Directions for Single Meal

1. Place the peeled and deveined shrimp into the base of the slow cooker. Add the butter, worcestershire sauce, minced garlic and BBQ sauce and toss gently.
2. Set the slow cooker on low and cook for 1 hour.
3. Warm the loaf bread.
4. Prepare the veggies.
5. Serve Slow Cooker BBQ Shrimp with a lemon wedge garnish and a side of bread and veggies.

Freezeasy Meal Prep Directions

- To each freezer bag, add the following ingredients:
  - 2 lbs. peeled deveined shrimp
  - 3 Tbsp butter
  - 3 Tbsp worcestershire sauce
  - 2 tsp minced garlic
  - 1 cup BBQ sauce
  - Salt and pepper
- Remove as much air as possible and seal. Add label to baggie and freeze.

Freeze & Thaw Instructions

Put baggie in the freezer and freeze up to 6 months in fridge freezer or 12 months in a deep freezer. Thaw in the fridge overnight, or a warm bowl of water for about 20 minutes, before transferring to the slow cooker and cooking on low for 1 hour.

Slow Cooker Lemon & Dill Salmon

Yield: 4 servings
Prep Time: 10 minutes
Cook Time: 1 hour in slow cooker

Ingredients for Single Meal

- 1 lb. salmon fillet
- Salt and pepper
- 2 tsp lemon juice
- 2 tsp fresh dill
- Side: veggies
- Side: rice
- 1 gallon-size freezer baggie

Cooking Directions for Single Meal

1. Place a large piece of parchment paper into the base of the slow cooker. The parchment paper is to make it easier to lift the salmon out of the slow cooker after it cooks.
2. Place the 4 salmon fillets flat on the parchment paper, skin side down. Sprinkle each with little salt and pepper over the top. Drizzle lemon juice over the salmon pieces. Place fresh chopped dill sprigs on salmon.
3. Set on high and cook for 1 hour.
4. Cook rice as directed on package.
5. Prepare veggies, as needed.
6. Once salmon is cooked, carefully lift it out of the slow cooker onto a shallow serving dish. Remove skin and serve.
7. Serve Lemon & Dill Salmon with rice and veggies.

Freezeasy Meal Prep Directions

- Cut 1 lb. salmon into 4 - 1/4 lb. fillets.
- Halve 2 lemons.
- Finely chop 2 tsp fresh dill.
- To gallon-size plastic freezer baggie, add the following ingredients:
  - Salmon fillets
  - Salt and pepper
  - Juice from 2 lemons
  - Chopped dill
- Remove as much air as possible and seal. Add label to baggie and freeze.

Freeze & Thaw Instructions

Put baggie in the freezer and freeze up to 6 months in fridge freezer or 12 months in a deep freezer. Thaw in the fridge overnight, or a warm bowl of water for about 20 minutes, before transferring to the slow cooker lined with parchment paper, and cooking on high for 1 hour.

Slow Cooker Red Curry with Cod

Yield: 4 servings
Prep Time: 15 minutes
Cook Time: 2 hours in slow cooker

Ingredients for Single Meal

- 2 - 15 oz. cans light coconut milk
- 3 Tbsp red curry paste
- 1 Tbsp curry powder
- 1 tsp ground ginger
- 1 tsp garlic powder
- 1 red bell pepper
- 12 oz. bag julienned carrot
- 1 lb. cod fish fillet
- Salt and pepper
- Garnish: cilantro and green onion
- Side: rice
- 1 gallon-size freezer baggie

Cooking Directions for Single Meal

1. To the slow cooker insert, add the cans of coconut milk and whisk in the curry paste, curry powder, ground ginger and garlic powder. Gently stir in the sliced bell peppers, julienned carrots and whole cod fillet.
2. Set on low and cook on high for 2 hours. Once finished cooking, gently pull the fish apart into bite size pieces. Season with salt and pepper to taste.
3. Cook rice, as directed.
4. Prepare optional garnish.
5. Serve Slow Cooker Red Curry with Cod over rice with cilantro and green onion garnish.

Freezeasy Meal Prep Directions

- Slice 1 red bell pepper.
- Open 2 cans of coconut milk.
- Whisk together 2 cans of light coconut milk, 3 Tbsp red curry paste, 1 Tbsp curry powder, 1 tsp ground ginger, and 1 tsp garlic powder.
- To gallon-size plastic freezer baggie, add the following ingredients:
  - 1 lb. cod fillet
  - 12 oz. bag julienned carrots or "matchstick" carrots
  - Sliced red bell peppers
  - Prepared curry sauce
- Remove as much as air as possible and seal.

Freeze & Thaw Instructions

Put baggie in the freezer and freeze up to 6 months in fridge freezer or 12 months in a deep freezer. Thaw in the fridge overnight, or a warm bowl of water for about 20 minutes, before transferring to the slow cooker and cooking on high for 2 hours. Once finished cooking, gently pull the fish apart into bite size pieces.

Slow Cooker Sesame Salmon

Yield:	4 servings
Prep Time:	10 minutes
Cook Time:	2 hours in slow cooker

Ingredients for Single Meal

- 1 lb. salmon fillet
- 3 Tbsp honey
- 2 Tbsp soy sauce
- 1 Tbsp sesame oil
- 1 tsp minced garlic
- 1 tsp ground ginger
- 1/2 tsp cayenne pepper
- Garnish: sesame seeds and green onions
- Side: rice
- Side: veggies
- 1 gallon-size freezer baggie
- 1 piece of parchment paper

Cooking Directions for Single Meal

1. Cut salmon into individual portions. Place the parchment paper into the base of the slow cooker and add the salmon fillets onto the parchment paper.
2. In a small bowl, whisk together the honey, soy sauce, sesame oil, minced garlic, ground ginger and cayenne pepper. Pour over the salmon, like a glaze.
3. Set the slow cooker on low and cook for 1 to 2 hours, or until salmon is cooked through. Check after 1 hour and continue slow cooking until finished cooking through. When serving, garnish with sesame seeds and sliced green onions.
4. Cook the rice, as directed.
5. Prepare veggies.
6. Serve Slow Cooker Sesame Salmon with rice and veggies.

Freezeasy Meal Prep Directions

- Cut 1 lb. salmon fillet into 4 individual serving portions.
- In a small bowl, whisk together 3 Tbsp honey, 2 Tbsp soy sauce, 1 Tbsp sesame oil, 1 tsp minced garlic, 1 tsp ground ginger and 1/2 tsp cayenne pepper.
- To gallon-size plastic freezer baggie, add the following ingredients:
  - Individual portion salmon fillets
  - Prepared marinade-glaze
- Remove as much air as possible and seal. Add label to baggie and freeze.

Freeze & Thaw Instructions

Put baggie in the freezer and freeze up to 6 months in fridge freezer or 12 months in a deep freezer. Thaw in the fridge overnight, or a warm bowl of water for about 20 minutes, before transferring to a parchment lined slow cooker and cooking on low for 2 hours.

Freezer to Slow Cooker Vegetarian Recipes

Slow Cooker Creamy Tortellini Soup

Slow Cooker Curried Chickpeas & Vegetables

Slow Cooker Minestrone Soup

Slow Cooker Pasta E Fagioli Soup

Slow Cooker Spanish Rice

Slow Cooker Tomato Basil Tortellini Soup

Slow Cooker Vegetable & Bean Soup

Slow Cooker Creamy Tortellini Soup

Yield:	4 servings
Prep Time:	10 minutes
Cook Time:	4 hours in slow cooker

Ingredients for Single Meal

- 2 whole carrots
- 2 celery stalk
- 1 small white onion
- 15 oz. can diced tomatoes
- 4 cups vegetable stock
- 2 tsp garlic powder
- 1 tsp Italian seasoning
- 20 oz. box cheese tortellini
- 1 cup heavy cream
- 1 cup milk
- 1/2 cup all purpose flour
- 1 cup grated Parmesan cheese
- 1 cup mozzarella cheese
- Garnish: chopped basil
- Side: salad
- 1 gallon-size freezer baggie

Cooking Directions for Single Meal

1. Peel and chop the carrots. Chop the celery. Chop the onion.
2. Open the diced tomatoes.
3. Place the chopped carrots, celery and onion, diced tomatoes and vegetable stock into the base of the slow cooker. Add the garlic powder, Italian seasoning with pinch of salt and pepper. Set the slow cooker on low and cook for 4 hours.
4. With 20 to 30 minutes left in the cooking cycle, whisk together the milk, cream and flour. Stir into the soup and add the cheese tortellini as well. Stir in the Parmesan and mozzarella cheeses. Let the cooking cycle finish and the ladle soup into bowls and garnish with fresh basil. Do not leave tortellini cooking or on warm mode in your slow cooker, so it doesn't overcook.
5. Prepare the salad.
6. Serve Slow Cooker Creamy Tortellini Soup with salad.

Freezeasy Meal Prep Directions

- Peel and chop 2 whole carrots. Chop 2 celery stalks. Chop 1 onion.
- Open 1 can of diced tomatoes.
- To gallon-size plastic freezer baggie, add the following ingredients:
  - Chopped carrots
  - Chopped celery
  - Chopped onion
  - 1 - 15 oz. can diced tomatoes
  - 2 tsp garlic powder
  - 1 tsp Italian seasoning
- Do NOT freeze the tortellini with other ingredients. It can be frozen in the box it comes in, and thawed the day you wish to make this meal.
- The milk, cream, flour and cheeses will be added at the end of cooking cycle. Do not add to freezer bag.
- Remove as much air as possible and seal. Add label to baggie and freeze.

Freeze & Thaw Instructions

Put baggie in the freezer and freeze up to 6 months in fridge freezer or 12 months in a deep freezer. Thaw in the fridge overnight, or a warm bowl of water for about 20 minutes, before transferring to the slow cooker and cooking on low for 4 hours. With 20 to 30 minutes left in the cooking cycle, stir in the milk, cream, flour, cheeses and tortellini as directed.

Slow Cooker Curried Chickpeas & Vegetables

Yield:	4 servings
Prep Time:	10 minutes
Cook Time:	8 hours in slow cooker

Ingredients for Single Meal

- 15 oz. can chickpeas
- 3 medium sweet potatoes
- 4 whole carrots
- 15 oz. can sweet peas
- 2 cups vegetable broth
- 1 Tbsp curry powder
- 1 tsp garlic powder
- 1 tsp ground ginger
- Salt and pepper
- Garnish: bunch cilantro
- Side: veggies
- 1 gallon-size freezer baggie

Cooking Directions for Single Meal

1. Peel and dice the sweet potatoes. Peel and slice the carrots.
2. Add all the ingredients except the garnish and sides to the slow cooker and add 2 cups of water. Set the slow cooker on low and cook for 8 hours.
3. Prepare veggies.
4. Serve Slow Cooker Curried Chickpeas & Vegetables with a side of fresh veggies.

Freezeasy Meal Prep Directions

- Peel and dice 3 sweet potatoes.
- Peel and slice 4 whole carrots.
- Open and drain 1 can of chickpeas. Open and drain 1 can of sweet peas.
- To gallon-size plastic freezer baggie, add the following ingredients:
  - Can of chickpeas
  - Diced sweet potatoes
  - Sliced carrots
  - Can of peas
  - 2 cups vegetable broth
  - 1 Tbsp curry powder
  - 1 tsp ground ginger
  - 1 tsp garlic powder
  - Salt and pepper to taste
- Remove as much as air as possible and seal.

Freeze & Thaw Instructions

Put baggie in the freezer and freeze up to 6 months in fridge freezer or 12 months in a deep freezer. Thaw in the fridge overnight, or a warm bowl of water for about 20 minutes, before transferring to the slow cooker and cooking on low for 8 hours.

Slow Cooker Minestrone Soup

Yield:	4 servings
Prep Time:	20 minutes
Cook Time:	8 hours in slow cooker

Ingredients for Single Meal

- 1 small white onion
- 2 celery stalks
- 2 garlic cloves
- 4 whole carrots
- 1/2 lb. green beans
- 15 oz. can tomato sauce
- 15 oz. can kidney beans
- 1 Tbsp Italian seasoning
- 6 cups vegetable stock
- Salt and pepper
- 1 1/2 cup elbow pasta noodles
- Garnish: Parmesan cheese
- Side: dinner rolls
- 1 gallon-size freezer baggie

Cooking Directions for Single Meal

1. Chop the onion and slice the celery. Peel and chop the carrots. Trim the green beans. Crush the garlic cloves.
2. Open, drain, and rinse the red kidney beans. Open the tomato sauce.
3. To the slow cooker, add the chopped onion, sliced celery, crushed garlic cloves, chopped carrots, green beans, tomato sauce, kidney beans, Italian seasoning and vegetable stock. Set on low and cook for 8 hours. Season with salt and pepper, as needed.
4. With 30 minutes left in the cooking cycle, stir in the pasta and let it cook through.
5. Warm the dinner rolls.
6. To keep the pasta from overcooking, ladle the soup into serving bowls right away.
7. Serve Slow Cooker Minestrone Soup with optional Parmesan cheese and side of dinner rolls.

Freezeasy Meal Prep Directions

- Chop 1 white onion.
- Peel and chop 4 whole carrots.
- Slice 2 celery stalks.
- Trim 1/2 lb. green beans, if needed.
- Open, drain and rinse 1 can of red kidney beans.
- Open 1 can of tomato sauce.
- To gallon-size plastic freezer baggie, add the following ingredients:
  - Chopped onion
  - Sliced celery
  - Crushed garlic cloves
  - Chopped carrots
  - Trimmed green beans
  - 15 oz. can tomato sauce
  - 15 oz. can red kidney beans
  - 1 Tbsp Italian seasoning blend
  - 6 cups vegetable stock (you could add this at the time of cooking if the freezer bag gets too full.)
- Do not add pasta to freezer meal baggie.
- Remove as much air as possible and seal. Add label to baggie and freeze.

Freeze & Thaw Instructions

Put baggie in the freezer and freeze up to 6 months in fridge freezer or 12 months in a deep freezer. Thaw in a warm bowl of water for about 20 minutes, before transferring all the ingredients to slow cooker. Set on low and cook for 8 hours. WIth 30 minutes left in the cooking cycle, stir in the pasta as directed.

Slow Cooker Pasta E Fagioli Soup

Yield: 4 servings
Prep Time: 10 minutes
Cook Time: 8 hours in slow cooker

Ingredients for Single Meal

- 1 small white onion
- 2 celery stalk
- 4 whole carrots
- 15 oz. can diced tomatoes
- 15 oz. can Cannellini beans
- 3 cups vegetable stock
- 2 tsp dried basil
- 1 tsp garlic powder
- Salt and pepper
- 12 oz. box elbow pasta noodles
- Garnish: shredded Parmesan cheese
- Side: salad
- 1 gallon-size freezer baggie

Cooking Directions for Single Meal

1. Chop the onion. Slice the celery. Peel and slice the carrots.
2. Open, drain, and rinse the Cannellini beans.
3. Add all the ingredients to the slow cooker except the pasta and garnish. Set slow cooker on low and cook for 8 hours.
4. When there is 30 minutes left in the cooking cycle, add the pasta plus 1 cup of hot water. (Note: You might need to add a little more liquid than the 1 cup, depending on how much liquid is already in there. The pasta will soak up about 2 cups of liquid.)
5. Prepare the salad.
6. Serve Slow Cooker Pasta E Fagioli Soup with Parmesan cheese garnish and salad.

Freezeasy Meal Prep Directions

- Chop 1 white onion. Slice 2 celery stalks. Peel and slice 4 carrots.
- Open, drain and rinse 1 can of Cannellini beans.
- Open 1 can of diced tomatoes.
- To gallon-size plastic freezer baggie, add the following ingredients:
  - Diced onion
  - Sliced celery
  - Sliced carrots
  - Can of diced tomatoes
  - Can of Cannellini beans
  - 3 cups vegetable stock
  - 2 tsp dried basil
  - 1 tsp garlic powder
  - Salt and pepper
- Do not add pasta to freezer meal baggie.
- Remove as much air as possible and seal. Add label to baggie and freeze.

Freeze & Thaw Instructions

Put baggie in the freezer and freeze up to 6 months in fridge freezer or 12 months in a deep freezer. Thaw in the fridge overnight, or a warm bowl of water for about 20 minutes, before transferring to the slow cooker and cooking on low for 8 hours. Stir in pasta with 1 cup of water with 30 minutes left in cooking cycle.

Slow Cooker Spanish Rice

Yield: 4 servings
Prep Time: 10 minutes
Cook Time: 3 hours in slow cooker

Ingredients for Single Meal

- 1 lb. uncooked brown rice
- 4 cups water
- 2 cups frozen chopped onion
- 2 cups frozen chopped green peppers
- 1 tsp minced garlic
- 2 tsp chili powder
- 2 tsp ground cumin
- 1 tsp dried oregano
- Salt and pepper
- 15 oz. can crushed tomatoes
- Side: veggies
- Side: avocado
- 1 gallon-size freezer baggie

Cooking Directions for Single Meal

1. Place the brown rice and water into the base of the slow cooker. Stir in the chopped onion, chopped green peppers, minced garlic, chili powder, ground cumin, oregano and salt and pepper in with the rice. Pour the crushed tomatoes with juices on top.
2. Set on low and cook for 2 to 3 hours. Fluff with a fork before serving.
3. Prepare veggies and slice the avocado.
4. Serve Slow Cooker Spanish Rice with veggies and sliced avocado.

Freezeasy Meal Prep Directions

- To gallon-size plastic freezer baggie, add the following ingredients:
  - 1 lb. uncooked brown rice
  - 2 cups frozen chopped onion
  - 2 cups frozen chopped green peppers
  - 1 tsp minced garlic
  - 2 tsp chili powder
  - 2 tsp ground cumin
  - 1 tsp dried oregano
  - Salt and pepper
- Note: Do NOT add water or crushed tomatoes to freezer bag.
- Remove as much air as possible and seal. Add label to baggie and freeze.

Freeze & Thaw Instructions

Put baggie in the freezer and freeze up to 6 months in fridge freezer or 12 months in a deep freezer. Thaw in the fridge overnight, or a warm bowl of water for about 20 minutes, before transferring to the slow cooker, adding 4 cups of water and crushed tomatoes on top, then cooking on low for 2 to 3 hours.

Slow Cooker Tomato Basil Tortellini Soup

Yield: 4 servings
Prep Time: 10 minutes
Cook Time: 1 hour in slow cooker

Ingredients for Single Meal

- 26 oz. jar spaghetti sauce
- 20 oz. box cheese tortellini
- 8 oz. box sliced white mushrooms
- 6 oz. bag fresh spinach
- 4 fresh basil leaves
- 1 Tbsp minced onion
- 1 tsp minced garlic
- 4 cups vegetable stock
- Salt and pepper
- Garnish: shredded Parmesan cheese
- Side: salad
- 1 gallon-size freezer baggie

Cooking Directions for Single Meal

1. Place all the ingredients, except the garnish and sides, into the base of the slow cooker and pour in 2 cups of hot water.
2. Set the slow cooker on low and cook for 1 hour, or until tortellini are tender. Once finished cooking, ladle soup into serving bowls immediately to keep the pasta from overcooking.
3. Prepare the salad.
4. Serve Tomato Basil Tortellini Soup with Parmesan cheese garnish and salad.

Freezeasy Meal Prep Directions

- To gallon-size plastic freezer baggie, add the following ingredients:
    - 26 oz. jar spaghetti sauce
    - 20 oz. box cheese tortellini
    - 8 oz. box sliced mushrooms
    - 6 oz. bag fresh spinach
    - 4 fresh basil leaves
    - 1 Tbsp minced onion
    - 1 tsp minced garlic
    - 4 cups vegetable stock
    - Salt and pepper
- Remove as much air as possible and seal. Add label to baggie and freeze.

Freeze & Thaw Instructions

Put baggie in the freezer and freeze up to 6 months in fridge freezer or 12 months in a deep freezer. Thaw in the fridge overnight, or a warm bowl of water for about 20 minutes, before transferring to the slow cooker and cooking on low for 1 hour.

Slow Cooker Vegetable & Bean Soup

Yield:	4 servings
Prep Time:	15 minutes
Cook Time:	8 hours in slow cooker

Ingredients for Single Meal

- 15 oz. can black beans
- 15 oz. can Cannellini beans
- 15 oz. can diced tomatoes
- 3 cups frozen mixed vegetables
- 1 Tbsp Italian seasoning
- 1 tsp garlic powder
- 3 cups vegetable stock
- Salt and pepper
- Side: dinner rolls
- 1 gallon-size freezer baggie

Cooking Directions for Single Meal

1. Open and drain the black beans and Cannellini beans.
2. Add all the ingredients to the slow cooker, except the dinner rolls. Set slow cooker on low and cook for 8 hours, or high for 4 hours.
3. Serve Slow Cooker Vegetable & Bean Soup with dinner rolls.

Freezeasy Meal Prep Directions

- Open, drain and rinse 1 can of black beans, and 1 can of Cannellini beans.
- Open 1 can of diced tomatoes.
- To gallon-size plastic freezer baggie, add the following ingredients:
  - Black beans, drained and rinsed
  - Cannellini beans, drained and rinsed
  - Diced tomatoes, undrained
  - 3 cups frozen mixed vegetables
  - 1 Tbsp Italian seasoning
  - 1 tsp garlic powder
  - 3 cups vegetable stock
  - Salt and pepper
- Remove as much air as possible and seal. Add label to baggie and freeze.

Freeze & Thaw Instructions

Put baggie in the freezer and freeze up to 6 months in fridge freezer or 12 months in a deep freezer. Thaw in the fridge overnight, or a warm bowl of water for about 20 minutes, before transferring to the slow cooker and cooking on low for 8 hours or high for 4 hours.

Freezer Meal Plan #1 With Shopping List

Slow Cooker BBQ Shrimp

Slow Cooker Caesar Pork Chops and Potatoes

Slow Cooker Creamy Ranch Chicken

Slow Cooker French Dip Sandwiches

Slow Cooker Jerk Pulled Pork Sliders

Note: The following meal plans are written with 5 recipes that double to make a total of 10 meals. The shopping lists and instructions are written to make 2 meals worth of each recipe.

1. Slow Cooker BBQ Shrimp

Yield: 4 servings
Active Time: 10 minutes. Cook Time: 1 hour in slow cooker

Recipe is written to make a single meal. Assembly Prep Directions & Shopping Lists will both contain directions and ingredients to make 2 meals, based on the number of servings you selected.

** This ingredient is used on the day you cook this meal. It is not added at the time you assemble and prepare your meals for the freezer.

Ingredients for Single Meal

- 2 - lb(s) peeled deveined shrimp
- 3 - Tbsp butter
- 3 - Tbsp Worcestershire sauce
- 2 - tsp minced garlic
- 1 - cup(s) BBQ sauce
- - Salt and pepper
- Garnish: - lemon wedges**
- Side: - French loaf bread**
- Side: - veggies**
- 1 - gallon-size freezer baggie(s)

Cooking Directions for Single Meal

1. Place the peeled and deveined shrimp into the base of the slow cooker. Add the butter, worcestershire sauce, minced garlic and BBQ sauce and toss gently.
2. Set the slow cooker on low and cook for 1 hour.
3. Warm the loaf bread.
4. Prepare the veggies.
5. Serve Slow Cooker BBQ Shrimp with a lemon wedge garnish and a side of bread and veggies.

Assembly Prep Directions for 2 Meals

- To each freezer bag, add the following ingredients:
  ○ 2 lbs. peeled deveined shrimp
  ○ 3 Tbsp butter
  ○ 3 Tbsp worcestershire sauce
  ○ 2 tsp minced garlic
  ○ 1 cup BBQ sauce
  ○ Salt and pepper
- Remove as much air as possible and seal. Add label to baggie and freeze.

Freeze & Thaw Instructions: *Put baggie in the freezer and freeze up to 6 months in fridge freezer or 12 months in a deep freezer. Thaw in the fridge overnight, or a warm bowl of water for about 20 minutes, before transferring to the slow cooker and cooking on low for 1 hour.*

Special Notes: *Make grits and enjoy a shrimp & grits night.*

Dairy-Free Modifications: *Recipe is dairy-free when made with dairy-free margarine.*

Gluten-Free Modifications: *Recipe is gluten-free when you serve with gluten-free sides.*

2. Slow Cooker Caesar Pork Chops and Potatoes

Yield: 4 servings
Active Time: 10 minutes. Cook Time: 8 hours in slow cooker

Recipe is written to make a single meal. Assembly Prep Directions & Shopping Lists will both contain directions and ingredients to make 2 meals, based on the number of servings you selected.

** This ingredient is used on the day you cook this meal. It is not added at the time you assemble and prepare your meals for the freezer.

Ingredients for Single Meal

- 4 - boneless pork chops
- - Salt and pepper
- 2 - lb(s) fingerling potatoes
- 1 - cup(s) Caesar salad dressing
- 1 packet - Italian seasoning
- Garnish: - shredded Parmesan cheese**
- Side: - salad**
- 1 - gallon-size freezer baggie(s)

Cooking Directions for Single Meal

1. Open the Italian seasoning packet and sprinkle into shallow dish or plate. Press both sides of the pork chops into the seasoning and then place into the the base of the slow cooker. Season with a little salt and pepper and then add the fingerling potatoes around the pork chops. Drizzle the Caesar dressing over the pork chops and potatoes.
2. Set the slow cooker on low and cook for 4 hours.
3. Prepare the salad.
4. Serve Slow Cooker Caesar Pork Chops and Potatoes with shredded Parmesan garnish and salad.

Assembly Prep Directions for 2 Meals

- Open 2 Italian seasoning packets and sprinkle into shallow dish or plate. Press both sides of the pork chops into the seasoning.
- To each gallon-size plastic freezer baggie, add the following ingredients:
  - 4 seasoned boneless pork chops
  - Salt and pepper
  - 1 - 2 lb. bag fingerling potatoes
  - 1 cup Caesar salad dressing
- Remove as much air as possible and seal. Add label to baggie and freeze.

Freeze & Thaw Instructions: *Put baggie in the freezer and freeze up to 6 months in fridge freezer or 12 months in a deep freezer. Thaw in the fridge overnight, or a warm bowl of water for about 20 minutes, before transferring to the slow cooker and cooking on low for 4 hours.*

Dairy-Free Modifications: *Unfortunately, there is not a great dairy-free option for this meal.*

Gluten-Free Modifications: *Recipe is gluten-free when served with gluten-free dressing and seasoning mix.*

3. Slow Cooker Creamy Ranch Chicken

Yield: 4 servings
Active Time: 20 minutes. Cook Time: 8 hours in slow cooker

Recipe is written to make a single meal. Assembly Prep Directions & Shopping Lists will both contain directions and ingredients to make 2 meals, based on the number of servings you selected.

** This ingredient is used on the day you cook this meal. It is not added at the time you assemble and prepare your meals for the freezer.

Ingredients for Single Meal

- 4 - Tbsp butter
- 4 - Tbsp all purpose flour
- 2 - cup(s) milk
- 1 - tsp salt
- To taste - pepper
- 4 - oz. baby bella mushrooms
- 2 - large boneless chicken breasts
- 1 - packet(s) ranch dressing mix
- 4 - oz. cream cheese
- Side: - dinner rolls**
- Side: - veggies**
- 1 - gallon-size freezer baggie(s)

Cooking Directions for Single Meal

1. Wash and chop the mushrooms.
2. In a large skillet or saucepan, melt the butter and then whisk in the flour. Whisking while pouring, add the milk to the flour-butter paste. Whisk milk in vigorously until the flour melts into the milk. Over medium heat, bring to bubbling and the sauce will begin to thicken. Add the salt and chopped mushrooms. {Let cool for 10-15 minutes if you are adding the sauce to the freezer bags during the all at once assembly of the packs.}
3. Place the chicken in the base of the slow cooker and season with salt and pepper and then add the ranch dressing mix over the top. Pour the homemade cream of mushroom soup over top of the chicken.
4. Set on low and cook for 8 hours. When there is 30 minutes left in the cooking cycle, switch the slow cooker to high and add the cream cheese and let it melt into the sauce.
5. Heat dinner rolls.
6. Prepare veggies.
7. Serve Creamy Ranch Chicken with dinner rolls and veggies.

Assembly Prep Directions for 2 Meals

- Wash and chop 8 oz. baby bella mushrooms.
- In a large skillet or saucepan, melt 8 Tbsp butter and then whisk in 8 Tbsp flour. Whisking while pouring, add 4 cups milk to the flour-butter paste. Whisk vigorously until the flour melts into the milk. Over medium heat, bring to bubbling and the sauce will begin to thicken. Add 2 tsp salt and the chopped mushrooms. Set aside and let cool.
- To each gallon-size plastic freezer baggie, add the following ingredients:
  - 2 large boneless skinless chicken breasts
  - 1 packet ranch dressing mix
  - Half of the prepared white sauce
  - (Note: let bag cool in the fridge before freezing.)
- Remove as much as air as possible and seal.

Freeze & Thaw Instructions: *Put baggie in the freezer and freeze up to 6 months in fridge freezer or 12 months in a deep freezer. Thaw in the fridge overnight, or a warm bowl of water for about 20 minutes, before transferring to the slow cooker and cooking on low for 8 hours. Stir in cream cheese at the end of cooking as directed.*

Special Notes: *Do NOT add cream cheese to freezer bag.*

Dairy-Free Modifications: *Unfortunately, there is not a simple dairy free modification for this meal.*

Gluten-Free Modifications: *Recipe is gluten-free when sauce made with gf flour & served with rice.*

4. Slow Cooker Teriyaki Chicken

Yield: 4 servings
Active Time: 10 minutes. Cook Time: 8 hours in slow cooker

Recipe is written to make a single meal. Assembly Prep Directions & Shopping Lists will both contain directions and ingredients to make 2 meals, based on the number of servings you selected.

** This ingredient is used on the day you cook this meal. It is not added at the time you assemble and prepare your meals for the freezer.

Ingredients for Single Meal

- 3 - lb(s) beef roast
- 1 - small white onion(s)
- 1 packet - dry French onion soup mix
- 1 - cup(s) beef broth
- - Salt and pepper
- 4 - slices Provolone cheese**
- 4 - bolillo or hoagie rolls**
- Side: - salad**
- 1 - gallon-size freezer baggie(s)

Cooking Directions for Single Meal

1. Slice the white onion.
2. Place the beef roast into the base of the slow cooker and add the sliced onions around the beef roast. Sprinkle the dry French onion soup mix around the beef and onions. Pour the beef stock around the edge of the slow cooker. Season with salt and pepper, as desired.
3. Set the slow cooker on low and cook for 8 hours. Once finished cooking, ladle out about 2 cups of the beef and onions to use as a dipping sauce. Then, slice or shred the beef roast and serve into the hoagie rolls. Add a slice of Provolone cheese to each sandwich.
4. Prepare the salad.
5. Serve Slow Cooker French Dip Sandwiches with salad.

Assembly Prep Directions for 2 Meals

- Slice 2 small white onions.
- To each gallon-size plastic freezer baggie, add the following ingredients:
  - 3 lb. beef roast
  - Half the sliced onions
  - 1 packet dry French onion soup mix
  - 1 cup beef broth
  - Salt and pepper
- Remove as much air as you can and seal. Freeze up to 6 months in your fridge freezer or 12 months in a deep freezer.

Freeze & Thaw Instructions: *Put baggie in the freezer and freeze up to 6 months in fridge freezer or 12 months in a deep freezer. Thaw in the fridge overnight, or a warm bowl of water for about 20 minutes, before transferring to the slow cooker and cooking on low for 8 hours. Assembly sandwiches and dip as directed.*

Dairy-Free Modifications: *Omit the Provolone cheese slices for dairy-free meal.*

Gluten-Free Modifications: *Unfortunately, there isn't a great gluten-free option for these sandwiches.*

5. Slow Cooker Jerk Pulled Pork Sliders

Yield: 4 servings
Active Time: 5 minutes. Cook Time: 8 hour in slow cooker

Recipe is written to make a single meal. Assembly Prep Directions & Shopping Lists will both contain directions and ingredients to make 2 meals, based on the number of servings you selected.

** This ingredient is used on the day you cook this meal. It is not added at the time you assemble and prepare your meals for the freezer.

Ingredients for Single Meal

- 2 - lb(s) pork roast
- - Salt and pepper
- 1/4 - cup(s) lime juice
- 3 - Tbsp Jerk seasoning
- 1 - tsp garlic powder
- 1 - tsp onion powder
- 1 - tsp ground cumin
- 1 - tsp brown sugar
- 1 - 8 oz. can sliced pineapple
- 12 - slider buns
- Garnish: - sliced green onions**
- Side: - fruit**
- Side: - chips**
- 1 - gallon-size freezer baggie(s)

Cooking Directions for Single Meal

1. Place the pork roast into the base of the slow cooker and season with salt and pepper. Pour the lime juice on and around the pork. Season with the Jerk seasoning, garlic powder, onion powder, ground cumin and brown sugar. Place the pineapple slices over the top.
2. Set the slow cooker on low and cook for 8 hours. Once finished cooking, shred the pork with 2 forks and mix into the sauce. Strain before adding the pork to the sliders.
3. Assemble sliders by adding the shredded pork and sliced green onion garnish.
4. Prepare fruit.
5. Serve Slow Cooker Jerk Pulled Pork Sliders with fruit and chips.

Assembly Prep Directions for 2 Meals

- Open and drain 2 cans of sliced pineapple.
- To each gallon-size plastic freezer baggie, add the following ingredients:
  - 2 lb. pork roast
  - Salt and pepper
  - 1/4 cup lime juice
  - 3 Tbsp Jerk seasoning
  - 1 tsp garlic powder
  - 1 tsp onion powder
  - 1 tsp ground cumin
  - 1 tsp brown sugar
  - 1 - 8 oz. can sliced pineapple
- Remove as much air as possible and seal. Add label to baggie and freeze.

Freeze & Thaw Instructions: *Put baggie in the freezer and freeze up to 6 months in fridge freezer or 12 months in a deep freezer. Thaw in the fridge overnight, or a warm bowl of water for about 20 minutes, before transferring to the slow cooker and cooking on low for 8 hours. Assemble sliders as directed.*

Dairy-Free Modifications: *Recipe is dairy-free when served with dairy-free sides.*

Gluten-Free Modifications: *Recipe is gluten-free when served with gluten-free sides like rice or lettuce cups.*

Complete Shopping List by Recipe

1. Slow Cooker BBQ Shrimp

- ☐ 4 lbs. peeled deveined shrimp
- ☐ 6 Tbsp butter
- ☐ 6 Tbsp Worcestershire sauce
- ☐ 4 tsp minced garlic
- ☐ 2 cups BBQ sauce
- ☐ Salt and pepper
- ☐ **Garnish:** lemon wedges
- ☐ **Side:** French loaf bread
- ☐ **Side:** veggies
- ☐ 2 gallon-size freezer baggies

2. Slow Cooker Caesar Pork Chops and Potatoes

- ☐ 8 boneless pork chops
- ☐ Salt and pepper
- ☐ 4 lbs. fingerling potatoes
- ☐ 2 cups Caesar salad dressing
- ☐ 2 Italian seasoning
- ☐ **Garnish:** shredded Parmesan cheese
- ☐ **Side:** salad
- ☐ 2 gallon-size freezer baggies

3. Slow Cooker Creamy Ranch Chicken

- ☐ 8 Tbsp butter
- ☐ 8 Tbsp all purpose flour
- ☐ 4 cups milk
- ☐ 2 tsp salt
- ☐ pepper
- ☐ 8 oz. baby bella mushrooms
- ☐ 4 large boneless chicken breasts
- ☐ 2 packets ranch dressing mix
- ☐ 8 oz. cream cheese
- ☐ **Side:** dinner rolls
- ☐ **Side:** veggies
- ☐ 2 gallon-size freezer baggies

4. Slow Cooker French Dip Sandwiches

- ☐ 6 lbs. beef roast
- ☐ 2 small white onions
- ☐ 2 dry French onion soup mix
- ☐ 2 cups beef broth
- ☐ Salt and pepper
- ☐ 8 slices Provolone cheese
- ☐ 8 bolillo or hoagie rolls
- ☐ **Side:** salad
- ☐ 2 gallon-size freezer baggies

5. Slow Cooker Jerk Pulled Pork Sliders

- ☐ 4 lbs. pork roast
- ☐ Salt and pepper
- ☐ 1/2 cups lime juice
- ☐ 6 Tbsp Jerk seasoning
- ☐ 2 tsp garlic powder
- ☐ 2 tsp onion powder
- ☐ 2 tsp ground cumin
- ☐ 2 tsp brown sugar
- ☐ 2 - 8 oz. can sliced pineapple
- ☐ 24 slider buns
- ☐ **Garnish:** sliced green onions
- ☐ **Side:** fruit
- ☐ **Side:** chips
- ☐ 2 gallon-size freezer baggies

Complete Shopping List by Store Section/Category

Meat

- ☐ 4 lbs. peeled deveined shrimp
- ☐ 8 boneless pork chops
- ☐ 4 large boneless chicken breasts
- ☐ 6 lbs. beef roast
- ☐ 4 lbs. pork roast

Produce

- ☐ **Garnish:** lemon wedges
- ☐ **Side:** veggies
- ☐ 4 lbs. fingerling potatoes
- ☐ **Side:** salad
- ☐ 8 oz. baby bella mushrooms
- ☐ 2 small white onions
- ☐ 1/2 cup lime juice
- ☐ **Garnish:** sliced green onions
- ☐ **Side:** fruit

Pantry Staples - Canned, Boxed

- ☐ 2 dry French onion soup mix
- ☐ 2 cups beef broth
- ☐ 2 - 8 oz. can sliced pineapple

Starchy Sides

- ☐ **Side:** French loaf bread
- ☐ **Side:** dinner rolls
- ☐ 8 bolillo or hoagie rolls
- ☐ 24 slider buns
- ☐ **Side:** chips

Sauces/Condiments

- ☐ 6 Tbsp Worcestershire sauce
- ☐ 2 cups BBQ sauce

Spices

- ☐ 4 tsp minced garlic
- ☐ Salt and pepper
- ☐ 2 cups Caesar salad dressing
- ☐ 2 Italian seasoning
- ☐ 8 Tbsp all purpose flour
- ☐ 2 tsp salt
- ☐ pepper
- ☐ 2 packets ranch dressing mix
- ☐ 6 Tbsp Jerk seasoning
- ☐ 2 tsp garlic powder
- ☐ 2 tsp onion powder
- ☐ 2 tsp ground cumin
- ☐ 2 tsp brown sugar

Dairy/Frozen

- ☐ 14 Tbsp butter
- ☐ **Garnish:** shredded Parmesan cheese
- ☐ 4 cups milk
- ☐ 8 oz. cream cheese
- ☐ 8 slices Provolone cheese

Supplies

- ☐ **Side:** 10 gallon-size freezer baggies

Freezer Meal Prep Day Shopping List by Recipe

1. Slow Cooker BBQ Shrimp

- ☐ 4 lbs. peeled deveined shrimp
- ☐ 6 Tbsp butter
- ☐ 6 Tbsp Worcestershire sauce
- ☐ 4 tsp minced garlic
- ☐ 2 cups BBQ sauce
- ☐ Salt and pepper
- ☐ 2 gallon-size freezer baggies

2. Slow Cooker Caesar Pork Chops and Potatoes

- ☐ 8 boneless pork chops
- ☐ Salt and pepper
- ☐ 4 lbs. fingerling potatoes
- ☐ 2 cups Caesar salad dressing
- ☐ 2 Italian seasoning
- ☐ 2 gallon-size freezer baggies

3. Slow Cooker Creamy Ranch Chicken

- ☐ 8 Tbsp butter
- ☐ 8 Tbsp all purpose flour
- ☐ 4 cups milk
- ☐ 2 tsp salt
- ☐ pepper
- ☐ 8 oz. baby bella mushrooms
- ☐ 4 large boneless chicken breasts
- ☐ 2 packets ranch dressing mix
- ☐ 8 oz. cream cheese
- ☐ 2 gallon-size freezer baggies

4. Slow Cooker French Dip Sandwiches

- ☐ 6 lbs. beef roast
- ☐ 2 small white onions
- ☐ 2 dry French onion soup mix
- ☐ 2 cups beef broth
- ☐ Salt and pepper
- ☐ 2 gallon-size freezer baggies

5. Slow Cooker Jerk Pulled Pork Sliders

- ☐ 4 lbs. pork roast
- ☐ Salt and pepper
- ☐ 1/2 cup lime juice
- ☐ 6 Tbsp Jerk seasoning
- ☐ 2 tsp garlic powder
- ☐ 2 tsp onion powder
- ☐ 2 tsp ground cumin
- ☐ 2 tsp brown sugar
- ☐ 2 - 8 oz. can sliced pineapple
- ☐ 24 slider buns
- ☐ 2 gallon-size freezer baggies

Freezer Meal Prep Day Shopping List by Store Section/Category

Note: This shopping list doesn't include any side dish items like fruit, dinner rolls, veggies or salad.

Meat

- ☐ 4 lbs. peeled deveined shrimp
- ☐ 8 boneless pork chops
- ☐ 4 large boneless chicken breasts
- ☐ 6 lbs. beef roast
- ☐ 4 lbs. pork roast

Produce

- ☐ 4 lbs. fingerling potatoes
- ☐ 8 oz. baby bella mushrooms
- ☐ 2 small white onions
- ☐ 1/2 cup lime juice

Pantry Staples - Canned, Boxed

- ☐ 2 dry French onion soup mix
- ☐ 2 cups beef broth
- ☐ 2 - 8 oz. can sliced pineapple

Starchy Sides

- ☐ 24 slider buns

Sauces/Condiments

- ☐ 6 Tbsp Worcestershire sauce
- ☐ 2 cups BBQ sauce

Spices

- ☐ 4 tsp minced garlic
- ☐ Salt and pepper
- ☐ 2 cups Caesar salad dressing
- ☐ 2 Italian seasoning
- ☐ 8 Tbsp all purpose flour
- ☐ 2 tsp salt
- ☐ pepper
- ☐ 2 packets ranch dressing mix
- ☐ 6 Tbsp Jerk seasoning
- ☐ 2 tsp garlic powder
- ☐ 2 tsp onion powder
- ☐ 2 tsp ground cumin
- ☐ 2 tsp brown sugar

Dairy/Frozen

- ☐ 14 Tbsp butter
- ☐ 4 cups milk
- ☐ 8 oz. cream cheese

Supplies

- ☐ 10x gallon-size freezer baggies

Meal Assembly Instructions

- ☐ Label your bags/foil with printable labels or sharpie.
- ☐ Pull out all the ingredients into a central location or into stations.

Pre-Cook & Chop Instructions

- ☐ Slice 2 small white onions.
- ☐ Wash and chop 8 oz. baby bella mushrooms.
- ☐ Open 2 Italian seasoning packets and sprinkle into shallow dish or plate. Press both sides of the pork chops into the seasoning.
- ☐ In a large skillet or saucepan, melt 8 Tbsp butter and then whisk in 8 Tbsp flour. Whisking while pouring, add 4 cups milk to the flour-butter paste. Whisk vigorously until the flour melts into the milk. Over medium heat, bring to bubbling and the sauce will begin to thicken. Add 2 tsp salt and the chopped mushrooms. Set aside and let cool.
- ☐ Open and drain 2 cans of sliced pineapple.

The Assembly Prep should take between 30 to 35 minutes.

Assembly by Recipe (Set Out on the Counter)

If you prefer to load your freezer baggies and trays one recipe at a time, you can follow the below instructions.

Slow Cooker BBQ Shrimp

To each freezer bag, add the following ingredients:

- 2 lbs. peeled deveined shrimp
- 3 Tbsp butter
- 3 Tbsp worcestershire sauce
- 2 tsp minced garlic
- 1 cup BBQ sauce
- Salt and pepper

Remove as much air as possible and seal. Add label to baggie and freeze.

Slow Cooker Caesar Pork Chops and Potatoes

To each gallon-size plastic freezer baggie, add the following ingredients:

- 4 seasoned boneless pork chops
- Salt and pepper
- 1 - 2 lb. bag fingerling potatoes
- 1 cup Caesar salad dressing

Remove as much air as possible and seal. Add label to baggie and freeze.

Slow Cooker Creamy Ranch Chicken

To each gallon-size plastic freezer baggie, add the following ingredients:

- 2 large boneless skinless chicken breasts
- 1 packet ranch dressing mix
- Half of the prepared white sauce
- (Note: let bag cool in the fridge before freezing.)

Remove as much as air as possible and seal.

Slow Cooker French Dip Sandwiches

To each gallon-size plastic freezer baggie, add the following ingredients:

- 3 lb. beef roast
- Half the sliced onions
- 1 packet dry French onion soup mix
- 1 cup beef broth
- Salt and pepper

Remove as much air as you can and seal. Freeze up to 6 months in your fridge freezer or 12 months in a deep freezer.

Slow Cooker Jerk Pulled Pork Sliders

To each gallon-size plastic freezer baggie, add the following ingredients:

- 2 lb. pork roast
- Salt and pepper
- 1/4 cup lime juice
- 3 Tbsp Jerk seasoning
- 1 tsp garlic powder
- 1 tsp onion powder
- 1 tsp ground cumin
- 1 tsp brown sugar
- 1 - 8 oz. can sliced pineapple

Remove as much air as possible and seal. Add label to baggie and freeze.

Freezer Meal Plan #2 With Shopping List

Slow Cooker Beef Stroganoff

Slow Cooker Cheesy Garlic Pork Chops

Slow Cooker Minestrone Soup

Slow Cooker Salsa Verde Pork Tacos

Slow Cooker Shredded Hawaiian Chicken Sandwiches

Note: The following meal plans are written with 5 recipes that double to make a total of 10 meals. The shopping lists and instructions are written to make 2 meals worth of each recipe.

1. Slow Cooker Beef Stroganoff

Yield: 4 servings
Active Time: 10 minutes. Cook Time: 8 hours in slow cooker

Recipe is written to make a single meal. Assembly Prep Directions & Shopping Lists will both contain directions and ingredients to make 2 meals, based on the number of servings you selected.

** This ingredient is used on the day you cook this meal. It is not added at the time you assemble and prepare your meals for the freezer.

Ingredients for Single Meal

- 1 - lb(s) ground beef
- 1 - Tbsp minced onion
- 1 - tsp garlic powder
- 1 - cup(s) beef broth
- 1 - tsp paprika
- 1 - 10 oz can(s) cream of mushroom
- - Salt and pepper
- 1 - cup(s) sour cream**
- Side: - egg noodles**
- Side: - veggies**
- 1 - gallon-size freezer baggie(s)

Cooking Directions for Single Meal

1. In a large skillet, brown the ground beef with the minced onion and garlic powder. Add the browned ground beef into the base of the slow cooker.
2. Stir in 1 cup beef broth, then sprinkle the paprika and combine with the meat and broth. Pour the cream of mushroom soup over the top and sprinkle with salt and pepper.
3. Set the slow cooker on low and cook for 8 hours. Just before serving, stir in 1 cup sour cream into the beef mixture.
4. Cook the egg noodles, as directed.
5. Prepare veggies.
6. Serve Slow Cooker Beef Stroganoff over egg noodles with veggies.

Assembly Prep Directions for 2 Meals

- Brown 2 lbs. ground beef with 2 Tbsp minced onion and 2 tsp garlic powder. Drain and set aside to cool.
- Open 2 cans of cream of mushroom soup.
- To each gallon-size plastic freezer baggie, add the following ingredients:
  - Half of the browned ground beef, cooled
  - 1 cup beef broth
  - 1 tsp paprika
  - Half of the canned cream of mushroom soup
- Remove as much air as possible and seal. Add label to baggie and freeze.

Freeze & Thaw Instructions: *Put baggie in the freezer and freeze up to 6 months in fridge freezer or 12 months in a deep freezer. Thaw in the fridge overnight, or a warm bowl of water for about 20 minutes, before transferring to the slow cooker and cooking on low for 8 hours. Just before serving, stir in 1 cup of sour cream.*

Special Notes: *If you wish to make your own cream of mushroom soup, visit 5dollardinners.com and search "homemade cream of mushroom sauce."*

Dairy-Free Modifications: *Unfortunately, there is not a great option for dairy-free meal.*

Gluten-Free Modifications: *Recipe is gluten-free when served over gluten-free pasta and homemade cream of mushroom sauce.*

2. Slow Cooker Cheesy Garlic Pork Chops

Yield: 4 servings
Active Time: 5 minutes. Cook Time: 4 hours in slow cooker

Recipe is written to make a single meal. Assembly Prep Directions & Shopping Lists will both contain directions and ingredients to make 2 meals, based on the number of servings you selected.

** This ingredient is used on the day you cook this meal. It is not added at the time you assemble and prepare your meals for the freezer.

Ingredients for Single Meal

- 4 - boneless pork chops
- - Salt and pepper
- 2 - Tbsp melted butter
- 2 - tsp minced garlic
- 1 - tsp onion powder
- 1 - cup(s) shredded mild cheddar cheese**
- Side: - dinner rolls**
- Side: - veggies**
- 1 - gallon-size freezer baggie(s)

Cooking Directions for Single Meal

1. Place the pork chops into the slow cooker insert and season with salt and pepper.
2. In a small bowl, stir the melted butter, minced garlic, and onion powder. Brush it onto the pork chops. Add a few pinchfuls of shredded mild cheddar cheese onto each pork chop.
3. Slow cook on low for 4 hours. Let rest for 5 minutes before serving or slicing. Cooking time may vary depending on thickness of the pork chops.
4. Prepare veggies.
5. Warm the dinner rolls.
6. Serve Slow Cooker Cheesy Garlic Pork Chops with veggies and dinner rolls.

Assembly Prep Directions for 2 Meals

- In a small bowl, stir 4 Tbsp melted butter, 4 tsp minced garlic, and 2 tsp onion powder.
- To each gallon size freezer baggie, add the following ingredients:
  - boneless pork chops
  - Melted butter mixture, brushed onto each pork chop
- Remove as much air as possible, add label and freeze.

Freeze & Thaw Instructions: *Put bag in the freezer and freeze up to 6 months in fridge freezer or 12 months in a deep freezer. Thaw in the fridge overnight, or a shallow dish of warm water for about 20 minutes, before transferring to the slow cooker, adding shredded cheese onto pork chops and cooking as directed.*

Dairy-Free Modifications: *Unfortunately, there isn't a great dairy-free option for this meal.*

Gluten-Free Modifications: *Recipe is gluten-free when served with gluten-free sides.*

3. Slow Cooker Minestrone Soup

Yield: 4 servings

Active Time: 20 minutes. Cook Time: 8 hours in slow cooker

Recipe is written to make a single meal. Assembly Prep Directions & Shopping Lists will both contain directions and ingredients to make 2 meals, based on the number of servings you selected.

** This ingredient is used on the day you cook this meal. It is not added at the time you assemble and prepare your meals for the freezer.

Ingredients for Single Meal

- 1 - small white onion(s)
- 2 - celery
- 2 - garlic cloves
- 4 - whole carrots
- 1/2 - lb(s) green beans
- 1 - 15 oz. can(s) tomato sauce
- 1 - 15 oz. can(s) kidney beans
- 1 - Tbsp Italian seasoning
- 6 - cup(s) chicken or vegetable stock
- - Salt and pepper
- 1 1/2 - cup(s) elbow pasta noodles**
- Garnish: - Parmesan cheese**
- Side: - dinner rolls**
- 1 - gallon-size freezer baggie(s)

Cooking Directions for Single Meal

1. Chop the onion and slice the celery. Peel and chop the carrots. Trim the green beans. Crush the garlic cloves.
2. Open, drain, and rinse the red kidney beans. Open the tomato sauce.
3. To the slow cooker, add the chopped onion, sliced celery, crushed garlic cloves, chopped carrots, green beans, tomato sauce, kidney beans, Italian seasoning and chicken stock. Set on low and cook for 8 hours. Season with salt and pepper, as needed.
4. With 30 minutes left in the cooking cycle, stir in the pasta and let it cook through.
5. Warm the dinner rolls.
6. To keep the pasta from overcooking, ladle the soup into serving bowls right away.
7. Serve Slow Cooker Minestrone Soup with optional Parmesan cheese and side of dinner rolls.

Assembly Prep Directions for 2 Meals

- Chop 2 white onions.
- Peel and chop 8 whole carrots.
- Slice 4 celery stalks.
- Trim 1 lb. green beans.
- Crush the garlic cloves.
- Open, drain and rinse 2 cans of red kidney beans.
- Open 2 cans of tomato sauce.
- To each gallon-size plastic freezer baggie, add the following ingredients:
  ○ Half of the chopped onion
  ○ Half of the sliced celery
  ○ Half of the crushed garlic cloves
  ○ Half of the chopped carrots
  ○ Half of the trimmed green beans
  ○ 1 - 15 oz. can tomato sauce
  ○ 1 - 15 oz. can red kidney beans, drained and rinsed
  ○ 1 Tbsp Italian seasoning blend
  ○ 6 cups chicken or vegetable stock or equivalent bouillon base plus water
- Remove as much air as possible and seal. Add label to baggie and freeze.

Freeze & Thaw Instructions: *Put baggie in the freezer and freeze up to 6 months in fridge freezer or 12 months in a deep freezer. Thaw in a warm bowl of water for about 20 minutes, before transferring all the ingredients to slow cooker. Set on low and cook for 8 hours. WIth 30 minutes left in the cooking cycle, stir in the pasta.*

Dairy-Free Modifications: *Recipe is dairy-free when served with dairy-free sides and when the Parmesan cheese garnish is omitted.*

Gluten-Free Modifications: *Use gluten-free small shell pasta noodles and serve with gluten free toast.*

4. Slow Cooker Salsa Verde Pork Tacos

Yield: 4 servings
Active Time: 10 minutes. Cook Time: 8 hours in slow cooker

Recipe is written to make a single meal. Assembly Prep Directions & Shopping Lists will both contain directions and ingredients to make 2 meals, based on the number of servings you selected.

** This ingredient is used on the day you cook this meal. It is not added at the time you assemble and prepare your meals for the freezer.

Ingredients for Single Meal

- 2 - lb(s) pork shoulder roast
- 1 - tsp garlic powder
- 1 - tsp ground cumin
- - Salt and pepper
- 1 1/2 - cup(s) salsa verde sauce
- 1 - large jalapeño(s)
- 12 - corn tortillas
- Garnish: - crumbled goat cheese**
- Garnish: - sour cream**
- Topping: - jalapeño(s)**
- Topping: - cilantro or avocado chunks**
- Side: - veggies**
- 1 - gallon-size freezer baggie(s)

Cooking Directions for Single Meal

1. Place the pork roast into the base of the slow cooker and sprinkle the garlic powder, ground cumin, salt and pepper on top of the pork roast. Pour the salsa verde and add the diced jalapenos on top.
2. Set the slow cooker on low and cook for 8 hours.
3. Once the cooking time is complete, shred the pork with 2 forks and remove from the slow cooker with slotted spoon when ready to serve. Spoon the shredded pork into the corn tortillas and add preferred toppings.
4. Prepare veggies.
5. Serve Salsa Verde Shredded Pork Tacos with veggies and preferred toppings.

Assembly Prep Directions for 2 Meals

- Remove the seeds and dice 2 jalapenos.
- To each gallon-size plastic freezer baggie, add the following ingredients:
  - 2 lb. pork shoulder roast
  - 1 tsp garlic powder
  - 1 tsp ground cumin
  - Salt and pepper
  - 1 1/2 cups salsa verde sauce
  - Half of the diced jalapeno into each bag
- Remove as much air as possible and seal. Add label to baggie and freeze.

Freeze & Thaw Instructions: *Put baggie in the freezer and freeze up to 6 months in fridge freezer or 12 months in a deep freezer. Thaw in a warm bowl of water for about 20 minutes, before transferring to the slow cooker and cooking on low for 8 hours.*

Dairy-Free Modifications: *Omit cheese or sour cream garnish.*

Gluten-Free Modifications: *Recipe is gluten-free when served with gluten-free sides.*

5. Slow Cooker Shredded Hawaiian Chicken Sandwiches

Yield: 4 servings
Active Time: 10 minutes. Cook Time: 8 hours in slow cooker

Recipe is written to make a single meal. Assembly Prep Directions & Shopping Lists will both contain directions and ingredients to make 2 meals, based on the number of servings you selected.

** This ingredient is used on the day you cook this meal. It is not added at the time you assemble and prepare your meals for the freezer.

Ingredients for Single Meal

- 1 - lb(s) boneless chicken breasts
- - Salt and pepper
- 1/4 - cup(s) BBQ sauce
- 1 - 8 oz. can(s) crushed pineapple
- 1/2 - small red onion(s)
- 4 - hamburger buns**
- Side: - chips**
- 1 - gallon-size freezer baggie(s)

Cooking Directions for Single Meal

1. Place the chicken breasts into the base of the slow cooker. Sprinkle a little salt and pepper over the top. Drizzle BBQ sauce over the chicken breasts and then pour the pineapple juices around the chicken breasts and the pineapple on top of the chicken.
2. (I like to add the onions raw after the chicken has cooked, but if you'd like to add them in while it all cooks, you can drop them in with the crushed pineapple.)
3. Set on low and cook for 8 hours.
4. Once cooked, pull out the chicken breasts and the pineapple and add to a bowl, then shred with 2 forks. Mix in the chopped red onion, if you didn't add it to the slow cooker.
5. Prepare fruit, as needed.
6. Serve Shredded Hawaiian Chicken Sandwiches with fruit and chips.

Assembly Prep Directions for 2 Meals

- Finely chop 1 small red onions.
- Open 2 cans of crushed pineapple. Do not drain.
- To each gallon-size plastic freezer baggie, add the following ingredients:
  - 1 lbs. boneless, skinless chicken breasts
  - Salt and pepper
  - About 1/4 cup BBQ sauce
  - Half of the canned pineapple, undrained
  - Half of the finely chopped onion
- Remove as much air as possible and seal. Add label to baggie and freeze.

Freeze & Thaw Instructions: *Put baggie in the freezer and freeze up to 6 months in fridge freezer or 12 months in a deep freezer. Thaw in the fridge overnight, or a warm bowl of water for about 20 minutes, before transferring to the slow cooker and cooking on low for 8 hours.*

Special Notes: *Use 1 lb. chicken breasts & 1 lb. chicken thighs, if you prefer a deeper flavor from the dark meat. Extra cooked, shredded chicken can be frozen to use in future meals.*

Dairy-Free Modifications: *Recipe is dairy-free when served with dairy-free sides.*

Gluten-Free Modifications: *Serve over rice instead of on buns, and serve with gluten-free chips.*

Complete Shopping List by Recipe

1. Slow Cooker Beef Stroganoff

- ☐ 2 lbs. ground beef
- ☐ 2 Tbsp minced onion
- ☐ 2 tsp garlic powder
- ☐ 2 cups beef broth
- ☐ 2 tsp paprika
- ☐ 2 - 10 oz. cans cream of mushroom
- ☐ Salt and pepper
- ☐ 2 cups sour cream
- ☐ **Side:** egg noodles
- ☐ **Side:** veggies
- ☐ 2 gallon-size freezer baggies

2. Slow Cooker Cheesy Garlic Pork Chops

- ☐ 8 boneless pork chops
- ☐ Salt and pepper
- ☐ 4 Tbsp melted butter
- ☐ 4 tsp minced garlic
- ☐ 2 tsp onion powder
- ☐ 2 cups shredded mild cheddar cheese
- ☐ **Side:** dinner rolls
- ☐ **Side:** veggies
- ☐ 2 gallon-size freezer baggies

3. Slow Cooker Minestrone Soup

- ☐ 2 small white onions
- ☐ 4 celery
- ☐ 4 garlic cloves
- ☐ 8 whole carrots
- ☐ 1 lb. green beans
- ☐ 2 - 15 oz. cans tomato sauce
- ☐ 2 - 15 oz. cans kidney beans
- ☐ 2 Tbsp Italian seasoning
- ☐ 12 cups chicken or vegetable stock
- ☐ Salt and pepper
- ☐ 3 cups elbow pasta noodles
- ☐ **Garnish:** Parmesan cheese
- ☐ **Side:** dinner rolls
- ☐ 2 gallon-size freezer baggies

4. Slow Cooker Salsa Verde Pork Tacos

- ☐ 4 lbs. pork shoulder roast
- ☐ 2 tsp garlic powder
- ☐ 2 tsp ground cumin
- ☐ Salt and pepper
- ☐ 3 cups salsa verde sauce
- ☐ 3 large jalapeños
- ☐ 24 corn tortillas
- ☐ **Garnish:** crumbled goat cheese
- ☐ **Garnish:** sour cream
- ☐ **Garnish:** jalapeños
- ☐ **Garnish:** cilantro or avocado chunks
- ☐ **Side:** veggies
- ☐ 2 gallon-size freezer baggies

5. Slow Cooker Shredded Hawaiian Chicken Sandwiches

- ☐ 2 lbs. boneless chicken breasts
- ☐ Salt and pepper
- ☐ 1/2 cup BBQ sauce
- ☐ 2 - 8 oz. cans crushed pineapple
- ☐ 1 small red onion
- ☐ 8 hamburger buns
- ☐ **Side:** chips
- ☐ 2 gallon-size freezer baggies

Complete Shopping List by Store Section/Category

Meat

- ☐ 2 lbs. ground beef
- ☐ 8 boneless pork chops
- ☐ 4 lbs. pork shoulder roast
- ☐ 2 lbs. boneless chicken breasts

Produce

- ☐ **Side:** veggies
- ☐ 2 small white onions
- ☐ 4 celery
- ☐ 8 whole carrots
- ☐ 1 lb. green beans
- ☐ 2 large jalapeños
- ☐ **Garnish:** jalapeños
- ☐ **Side:** cilantro or avocado chunks
- ☐ 1 small red onion

Pantry Staples - Canned, Boxed

- ☐ 2 cups beef broth
- ☐ 2 - 10 oz. cans cream of mushroom
- ☐ 2 - 15 oz. cans tomato sauce
- ☐ 2 - 15 oz. cans kidney beans
- ☐ 12 cups chicken or vegetable stock
- ☐ 3 cups elbow pasta noodles
- ☐ 2 - 8 oz. cans crushed pineapple

Starchy Sides

- ☐ **Side:** egg noodles
- ☐ **Side:** dinner rolls
- ☐ 24 corn tortillas
- ☐ 8 hamburger buns
- ☐ **Side:** chips

Sauces/Condiments

- ☐ 3 cups salsa verde sauce
- ☐ 1/2 cup BBQ sauce

Spices

- ☐ 2 Tbsp minced onion
- ☐ 4 tsp garlic powder
- ☐ 2 tsp paprika
- ☐ Salt and pepper
- ☐ 4 tsp minced garlic
- ☐ 2 tsp onion powder
- ☐ 4 garlic cloves
- ☐ 2 Tbsp Italian seasoning
- ☐ 2 tsp ground cumin

Dairy/Frozen

- ☐ 2 cups sour cream
- ☐ 2 cups shredded mild cheddar cheese
- ☐ **Side:** Parmesan cheese
- ☐ **Garnish:** crumbled goat cheese
- ☐ **Garnish:** sour cream

Supplies

- ☐ **Side:** 10 gallon-size freezer baggies
- ☐ 4 Tbsp melted butter

Freezer Meal Prep Day Shopping List by Recipe

Note: This shopping list doesn't include any side dish items like rice, dinner rolls, veggies or salad.
**In addition to a shopping list for prep day, this list could be used to help you organize ingredients on your counter before you begin preparing the meals for the freezer.

1. Slow Cooker Beef Stroganoff

- ☐ 2 lbs. ground beef
- ☐ 2 Tbsp minced onion
- ☐ 2 tsp garlic powder
- ☐ 2 cups beef broth
- ☐ 2 tsp paprika
- ☐ 2 - 10 oz. cans cream of mushroom
- ☐ Salt and pepper
- ☐ 2 gallon-size freezer baggies

2. Slow Cooker Cheesy Garlic Pork Chops

- ☐ 8 boneless pork chops
- ☐ Salt and pepper
- ☐ 4 Tbsp melted butter
- ☐ 4 tsp minced garlic
- ☐ 2 tsp onion powder
- ☐ 2 gallon-size freezer baggies

3. Slow Cooker Minestrone Soup

- ☐ 2 small white onions
- ☐ 4 celery
- ☐ 4 garlic cloves
- ☐ 8 whole carrots
- ☐ 1 lb. green beans
- ☐ 2 - 15 oz. cans tomato sauce
- ☐ 2 - 15 oz. cans kidney beans
- ☐ 2 Tbsp Italian seasoning
- ☐ 12 cups chicken or vegetable stock
- ☐ Salt and pepper
- ☐ 2 gallon-size freezer baggies

4. Slow Cooker Salsa Verde Pork Tacos

- ☐ 4 lbs. pork shoulder roast
- ☐ 2 tsp garlic powder
- ☐ 2 tsp ground cumin
- ☐ Salt and pepper
- ☐ 3 cups salsa verde sauce
- ☐ 2 large jalapeños
- ☐ 24 corn tortillas
- ☐ 2 gallon-size freezer baggies

5. Slow Cooker Shredded Hawaiian Chicken Sandwiches

- ☐ 2 lbs. boneless chicken breasts
- ☐ Salt and pepper
- ☐ 1/2 cup BBQ sauce
- ☐ 2 - 8 oz. cans crushed pineapple
- ☐ 1 small red onion
- ☐ 2 gallon-size freezer baggie

Freezer Meal Prep Day Shopping List by Store Section/Category

Note: *This shopping list doesn't include any side dish items like fruit, dinner rolls, veggies or salad.*

Meat

- ☐ 2 lbs. ground beef
- ☐ 8 boneless pork chops
- ☐ 4 lbs. pork shoulder roast
- ☐ 2 lbs. boneless chicken breasts

Produce

- ☐ 2 small white onions
- ☐ 4 celery
- ☐ 8 whole carrots
- ☐ 1 lb. green beans
- ☐ 2 large jalapeños
- ☐ 1 small red onion

Pantry Staples - Canned, Boxed

- ☐ 2 cups beef broth
- ☐ 2 - 10 oz. cans cream of mushroom
- ☐ 2 - 15 oz. cans tomato sauce
- ☐ 2 - 15 oz. cans kidney beans
- ☐ 12 cups chicken or vegetable stock
- ☐ 2 - 8 oz. cans crushed pineapple

Starchy Sides

- ☐ 24 corn tortillas

Sauces/Condiments

- ☐ 3 cups salsa verde sauce
- ☐ 1/2 cup BBQ sauce

Spices

- ☐ 2 Tbsp minced onion
- ☐ 4 tsp garlic powder
- ☐ 2 tsp paprika
- ☐ Salt and pepper
- ☐ 4 tsp minced garlic
- ☐ 2 tsp onion powder
- ☐ 4 garlic cloves
- ☐ 2 Tbsp Italian seasoning
- ☐ 2 tsp ground cumin

Supplies

- ☐ 10x gallon-size freezer baggie
- ☐ 4 Tbsp melted butter

Meal Assembly Instructions

☐ Label your bags/foil with printable labels or sharpie.
☐ Pull out all the ingredients into a central location or into stations.

Pre-Cook & Chop Instructions

☐ Brown 2 lbs. ground beef with 2 Tbsp minced onion and 2 tsp garlic powder. Drain and set aside to cool.
☐ Chop 2 white onions.
☐ Peel and chop 8 whole carrots.
☐ Slice 4 celery stalks.
☐ Trim 1 lb. green beans.
☐ Crush the garlic cloves.
☐ Remove the seeds and dice 2 jalapenos.
☐ Finely chop 1 small red onions.
☐ In a small bowl, stir 4 Tbsp melted butter, 4 tsp minced garlic, and 2 tsp onion powder.
☐ Open 2 cans of cream of mushroom soup.
☐ Open, drain and rinse 2 cans of red kidney beans.
☐ Open 2 cans of tomato sauce.
☐ Open 2 cans of crushed pineapple. Do not drain.

The Assembly Prep should take between 30 to 35 minutes.

Assembly by Recipe (Set Out on the Counter)

If you prefer to load your freezer baggies and trays one recipe at a time, you can follow the below instructions.

Slow Cooker Beef Stroganoff

To each gallon-size plastic freezer baggie, add the following ingredients:

- Half of the browned ground beef, cooled
- 1 cup beef broth
- 1 tsp paprika
- Half of the canned cream of mushroom soup

Remove as much air as possible and seal. Add label to baggie and freeze.

Slow Cooker Cheesy Garlic Pork Chops

To each gallon size freezer baggie, add the following ingredients:

- 4 boneless pork chops
- Melted butter mixture, brushed onto each pork chop

Remove as much air as possible, add label and freeze.

Slow Cooker Minestrone Soup

To each gallon-size plastic freezer baggie, add the following ingredients:

- Half of the chopped onion
- Half of the sliced celery
- Half of the crushed garlic cloves
- Half of the chopped carrots
- Half of the trimmed green beans
- 1 - 15 oz. can tomato sauce
- 1 - 15 oz. can red kidney beans, drained and rinsed
- 1 Tbsp Italian seasoning blend
- 6 cups chicken or vegetable stock or equivalent bouillon base plus water

Remove as much air as possible and seal. Add label to baggie and freeze.

Slow Cooker Salsa Verde Pork Tacos

To each gallon-size plastic freezer baggie, add the following ingredients:

- 2 lb. pork shoulder roast
- 1 tsp garlic powder
- 1 tsp ground cumin
- Salt and pepper
- 1 1/2 cups salsa verde sauce
- Half of the diced jalapeno into each bag

Remove as much air as possible and seal. Add label to baggie and freeze.

Slow Cooker Shredded Hawaiian Chicken Sandwiches

To each gallon-size plastic freezer baggie, add the following ingredients:

- 1 lbs. boneless, skinless chicken breasts
- Salt and pepper
- about 1/4 cup BBQ sauce
- Half of the canned pineapple, undrained
- Half of the finely chopped onion

Remove as much air as possible and seal. Add label to baggie and freeze.

Get More Freezer Meal Plans Like These!

MyFreezEasy allows you to create the perfect freezer meal plan, made up of recipes that you choose and that your family will love. Freezer meals save money on groceries, time in the kitchen and some stress at the dinner hour too.

Load up your freezer with make-ahead meals and dinnertime will be a breeze!

Don't forget to sign up for the free MyFreezEasy online workshop, you'll learn just about everything you need to know about freezer cooking and how it can transform your family's dinner experience.

Sign up for free at: www.myfreezeasy.com/workshop

FREE
Freezer Cooking
Online Workshop

GET STARTED

Made in the USA
Monee, IL
17 October 2020